Florida

Columbus Quincentenary Series

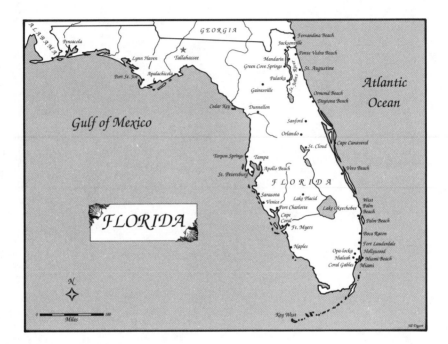

FLORIDA

A Short History

Revised Edition

Michael Gannon

University Press of Florida
Gainesville   Tallahassee   Tampa   Boca Raton
Pensacola   Orlando   Miami   Jacksonville   Ft. Myers

Library of Congress Cataloging in Publication Data
Gannon, Michael V.
   Florida: a short history / Michael Gannon.
      p.   cm.
   Includes bibliographical references and index.
   ISBN 0-8130-2681-4 (cloth).—ISBN 0-8130-2680-6 (paper)
   1. Florida–History.   I. Title.
F311.G34   1992   92-20714
975.9—dc20   CIP

Cover: *St. Augustine, 1890*, by Robert S. German, oil on canvas, 14 1/8 x 22. Courtesy of the Sam and Robbie Vickers Florida Collection. Map of Florida by Thomas Jefferys, 1775.

Picture credits appear on the page following the index.

The University Press of Florida is the scholarly publishing agency for the State University System of Florida, comprised of Florida A&M University, Florida Atlantic University, Florida Gulf Coast University, Florida International University, Florida State University, University of Central Florida, University of Florida, University of North Florida, University of South Florida, and University of West Florida.

University Press of Florida
15 Northwest 15th Street
Gainesville, FL 32611
http://www.upf.com

To My Students in Florida History at the
University of Florida, 1967–2003

CONTENTS

ACKNOWLEDGMENTS

I have many people to thank for assistance in the preparation of this volume, among them: George Bedell and Walda Metcalf, Director and Senior Editor, respectively, of the University Press of Florida, who first suggested that this narrative could stand as an independent book introducing Florida history to the general reader; Phillip L. Martin, who, in his capacity as director of the University of Florida Press, saw me through the initial editing; Judy Goffman, whose fine copyediting hand saved me from numerous slips and infelicitous expressions; the late Manning J. Dauer, Distinguished Service Professor of Political Science, who commissioned most of the first half of this narrative as a chapter in his edited volume, *Florida's Politics and Government* (Gainesville: University of Florida Press, 1980); Robert J. Huckshorn, Professor of Political Science and Associate Vice-President for Academic Affairs at Florida Atlantic University, who commissioned most of the second half of this narrative for his edited volume, *Government and Politics in Florida* (Gainesville: University of Florida Press, 1991); Elizabeth Alexander, Chair of the P.K. Yonge Library of Florida History at the University of Florida, and Archivist Bruce Chappell, also at the P.K. Yonge Library, whose unfailing assistance and courtesy made my research a pleasure; and Samuel Proctor, Distinguished Service Professor of History at the University of Florida, Editor of the *Florida Historical Quarterly*, dean of Florida historians, and my valued good friend who kindly read this narrative before publication (but who must be relieved of all responsibility for any mistakes in fact or interpretation). Numerous other history colleagues in the state of Florida have enlarged my understanding with their information, insights, and suggestions. A reading of both their published and unpublished works undergirds this entire effort.

A special thanks goes to my secretary, Myrna Sulsona, who, with her usual skill, transformed my manuscript into presentable form.

For the engravings, maps, and photographs that accompany the text I am indebted to Joan Morris and Joanna Norman, of the Photographic Collection, Florida State

Archives, in Tallahassee; Page Edwards and Kenneth Barrett, Jr., of the St. Augustine Historical Society; Paul Camp and Gary Mormino, of the Florida Historical Society Archives at the University of South Florida, Tampa; and Dawn Hugh of the Historical Association of Southern Florida, Miami.

To my spouse, Genevieve Haugen, who is relieved to know that I will now pick up the papers strewn across my study floor, goes the usual loving thanks.

Acknowledgments for the Revised Edition

Since its first publication ten years ago, this slim volume has enjoyed a wide readership throughout the state of Florida. Such acceptance is gratifying because it had been my hope from the beginning to place the story of Florida in as many hands as possible, at minimal cost.

The larger history of Florida promised on page xii was duly published as *The New History of Florida,* edited by Michael Gannon (Gainesville: University Press of Florida, 1996). In it the reader will find historical figures such as Barron Gift Collier, A. Philip Randolph, and Harry T. Moore, who, for lack of space, are missing in the present text.

Several knowledgeable readers have made suggestions for improvements in this text. I particularly thank Vernon Peeples, Catherine S. Manegold, and Paul S. George, as well as the many correspondents who caught the misspelling of Anton Cermak, mayor of Chicago (page 91).

The quip about the Pilgrims landing at Plymouth (page 4), which has been widely quoted, was originated by the late Father Leslie Cann, of the Diocese of Palm Beach, whom I am happy to acknowledge. The story of Ella Neill (pages 93–94) was confirmed to me in detail by the late B. K. Roberts, Tallahassee attorney and former chief justice of the Florida Supreme Court, who owned and lived in the apartment house where Miss Ella conducted much of the state's business.

Michael Gannon
Gainesville
January 1, 2003

INTRODUCTION

If you are one of the 16 million or so Floridians (or non-Floridians, for that matter) who know little or nothing of Florida's history, and would like to know something about it—but not that much!—then this book was written for you.

It is not a textbook. Relax. Consider it instead an *invitation* to Florida history.

Here is the basic story of America's peninsular state, told in short compass, written in what I hope is a fast-moving, attractive style.

Let me introduce our brief journey into the past with these reflections:

Many people seem to think that Florida's story began with the railroads and hotels of Henry M. Flagler a hundred years ago, or with the Florida land boom of the 1920s, or even with the Second World War, when, with its many military and naval bases, Florida became a garrison state (surrounded for a time by German U-boats).

No doubt Henry Flagler, with his desire to create an "American Riviera," abruptly brought Florida into the modern world.

And the 1920s, when millions of Americans by Model T flivver, train, or boat answered the call of overwrought promoters—"Florida," wrote one advertisement in northern papers, "is an emerald kingdom by southern seas, fanned by zephyrs laden with ozone from stately pines, watered by Lethe's copious libation, decked with palm and pine, flower and fern, clothed in perpetual verdure and lapt in the gorgeous folds of the semi-tropical zone"—were surely a watershed decade for raising national awareness of Florida's attributes and attractions. And indeed World War II was, as historians say, an "engine of social change" for Florida, since a large number of the millions of servicemen and -women who had trained here, and construction workers who had built bases, weapons, and cargo ships here, returned after 1945 to make Florida their home.

But Florida's history is much older and richer than all of that, as you will read. In fact, *Florida has the longest recorded history of any of the American states.* Its written record goes back to the time of men who, like its European discoverer Juan Ponce de León, had sailed with Christopher Columbus; to the time of Florida's first discoverers, residents, farmers, craftsmen, and developers, whom the Europeans called "Indians"; to the time of conquistadors and hidalgos who vainly hunted Florida for gold and silver; to the time of brave, resourceful women who created pioneer households in the subtropical wilderness; and to the time of gray-robed friars, whose missions stretched across Florida like rosary beads two centuries before the better-known missions of California. Florida was the cradle of our country and the first name of European origin to be etched upon its maps.

Florida participated in the major events of Spanish and English colonial history. It passed through and was shaped by the American Revolution and the Civil War. It reflected, in ways both large and small, the signal movements of national change and progress that took place in the last 100 years. And when it was ready to play its own distinct role in the development of the American story it leapt from being one of the least populated states at the start of World War II to the position of fourth most populated in 1992.

To tell the entire story (which I plan to do in another, larger volume) would require many more pages than you, the general reader, might have patience for at the present time. As William McClung, an editor with the University of California Press, said once about compact books such as this one, "The idea here is to persuade a scholar who would write a thousand pages to write the same thing, more or less, in a hundred pages. We have a responsibility to other scholars, but we also have a responsibility to those who simply want to know" (quoted in Wayne King, "University of California," *New York Times Book Review*, October 19, 1980, p. 43). Hence, I have chosen as a model for this slim work the highly successful and memorable *Florida Under Five Flags*, by the late Rembert W. Patrick, first published in

1945, and reprinted many times through the years, until it was clear to Dr. Patrick and his publisher that the book was out-of-date given the great amount of new research material that was becoming available.

Dr. Patrick's first edition was a tightly written narrative of 105 pages, "designed to be read in a short evening." For his purpose of introducing the field of Florida history to a general audience he was restrained, as I have been, from mentioning numerous important persons, places, and events that one would expect to see in a larger work. But he presented the essential outlines of the story, and that is what I have attempted to do here—keeping the focus always on Florida's *people*.

My hope is that you the reader will find in these few pages an inspiration to read more widely and deeply in the field of Florida history than this one short book allows. If you are a Florida resident, begin with your local history, however it exists, in book, booklet, pamphlet, or museum form. Every city and town in this state has a rich story to tell—of its people, its buildings and homes, its businesses, recreation, and culture. Beyond local history there is an abundance of general historical literature, much of it fascinating in the extreme. For your guidance I have provided at the end of this narrative a list of recommended volumes with which you might begin.

Every major city, and many small ones, in the state have a local historical association or society that you might consider joining. The members would warmly welcome you. There is also the statewide Florida Historical Society, which meets annually and publishes the nationally respected *Florida Historical Quarterly*. Many communities have historic preservation boards for the preservation and restoration of historic buildings, and Florida history museums, large and small, can be found throughout the state.

If it is true, as paleontologist Pierre Teilhard de Chardin has written, that everything is the sum of the past, and that nothing is understandable except through its history, then, it seems to me, all of us should grow into a deeper understanding of Florida's past. Everyday we are affected by what happened yesterday. Join me now in this short volume as together we take a somewhat rapid overview of the centuries and the decades.

In the Beginning

In the beginning was the land—warm, wet, and lush. The people poked holes in the land with pointed sticks and planted seeds of corn, beans, squash, and pumpkin. Under dense pine and oak canopies they hunted with the panther and ran with the deer. Along the shores and estuaries they consumed oysters, clams, and conchs, leaving behind vast heaps of shells. With spear and trap they fished the innumerable spring-fed rivers and streams. Across the crystalline waters women swam with children on their backs, while warriors, with bows and arrows of great accuracy and force, stood sentry against attack from neighboring tribes. Their residential communities were tree trunk-walled enclaves with guard gates. Some of their activity centers, called council houses, held as many as 2,500 persons at a time. Day and night huge fires spread the smoke that kept mosquitoes at bay, while witch doctors interpreted the fire pops for signs of war.

These were the first people of Florida. Called Panzacola, Chatot, and Apalachicola in the Panhandle, Apalachee where the land makes its great arching sweep south, Timucua in the north half of the peninsula, Calusa in the confederacy of tribes that inhabited the south, and Matecumbe in the Keys, these first residents of Florida descended from Eurasians who had crossed the ice bridge from Siberia to Alaska, perhaps 12,000 years ago. Those first discoverers and pioneers, traversing a continent on foot, entered a Florida that, 25 million years before, had begun the long process of emerging from the sea to become a green

These Timucuan inhabitants of north-central Florida were sketched and later painted by Jacques Le Moyne, who accompanied a French expedition to the mouth of the St. Johns River in 1564. Le Moyne's pictures are the only graphic depiction we have of the original Florida Indians. (The better-known Seminoles did not come into Florida until nearly two centuries later.) Here the artist shows women in Spanish moss garments and men in breechcloths with their hair trussed up in the shape of a bun. The seeds being planted are beans or maize (corn), says le Moyne, who adds that the Indians left their fields in the cold months, December 24 to March 15: "During this time the natives seek shelter in the woods, since they go naked. As soon as the cold winter is over, they return to their homes and wait for the crops to ripen."

wilderness of invincible beauty, hung low from the continent like fruit from a tree.

The indigenous tribes lived in close communion with the natural environment. The earth was their mother as well as their home. They wore a minimum of clothing, the men a deerskin breechcloth, the women a short skirt made from Spanish moss. Their world was one of birds, nearly 500 species, of lakes, more than 7,800, of a vast river of grass, the Everglades, of pine flatwoods, mixed hardwoods, saw palmetto and wiregrass, of salt marshes, cypress and custard apple swamps, scrub and dry prairies, golden beaches. Their god was the sun, which rose each morning in an orange explosion and began its beneficent journey across the blue dome of sky, bathing the land with re-birth and warmth.

The sun's ever-predictable reappearance was a sign in their lives of regularity and familiarity—until that incredible morning when off the shore the radiant orange light glanced off hulls and masts of broad black ships, many times larger than their own fire-dug canoes, and the seawind-filled canvas sails, the like of which these people had not seen before. To their aston-ishment, the strange white-faced men who debarked from those ships were from another stream of the same human family, one that had flowed for countless ages apart.

Some of the tribes would welcome these visitors and attempt to understand their curious ways. Most, understandably, saw them as a threat to their ownership of the fields and shores—and to the continuance of their way of life. Those tribes, then, filled their quivers with shell-tipped arrows and drank cacina, the tea of war.

They resisted, they struggled, they fought. But it was to no avail. With higher technologies, more sophisticated weapons, and (unknown to either side) major communicable diseases to which the indigenous people had no immunities, the visitors overcame, and a new culture, different in every respect from their own, took root in the ancient fields and shores.

European Settlement

Florida was Europe's first frontier in North America. Its history of permanent settlement by Europeans goes back over four and a quarter centuries. One would not know that fact, however, from reading the typical American his-tory textbook, even some used in Florida's own school sys-tems. According to the best-known accounts, Western civi-lization arrived in our country with the landing of the English at Jamestown in 1607 and at Plymouth Rock in 1620, but by the latter date Florida had long since been ex-plored and settled and the Spanish city of St. Augustine was fifty-five years old.

According to the documents, it was Juan Ponce de León, lately governor of Puerto Rico, who first happened onto this peninsula while searching for an island with rejuvenating waters. (Though unrecorded, Spanish slavers from Cuba probably preceded him.) The most recent estimate, based on a resailing of the voyage, is that Juan Ponce made his landfall south of Cape Canaveral, at or near Melbourne Beach. The date was Eastertime of 1513, and he named the place *La Florida*—"the Flowery Land." In the next fifty years, six expeditions, one of them French, either traversed the land or attempted to settle it. The last of these, directed by Spain's most experienced admiral, Pedro Menéndez de Avilés, succeeded in founding St. Augustine, which today proudly wears the mantle of the first permanent European settlement and oldest city in the continental United States. The year was 1565.

By the time the Pilgrims came ashore at Plymouth, St. Augustine was up for urban renewal. It was a town with fort, church, seminary, six-bed hospital, fish market, and about 120 shops and houses. Because *La Florida* stretched north from the Keys to Newfoundland and west to Texas, St. Augustine could claim to be the capital of much of what is now the United States. Though its territorial claims would shrink markedly over the next two hundred years, largely through English colonial encroachments, and though it would never know prosperity or power of the sort that could be found in Mexico and Peru, St. Augustine would nonetheless endure. The Spanish nation called it *la siempre fiel ciudad*, "the ever-faithful city." Except for twenty-one years under British rule, St. Augustine would salute the flag of Spain for nearly two and a half centuries. Not until the year 2055 will an American flag have flown over Florida as long as did the flag of Spain.

Menéndez's success in founding a settlement at St. Augustine came at the end of a long series of similar but unsuccessful attempts. Sir Walter Raleigh told the story of the early expeditions in his *History of the World*: "I cannot forbear to commend the patient virtue of the Spaniards. We seldom or never find that any nation hath endured so many misadventures and miseries as the Spaniards have done in their Indian discoveries. . . . Yea more than one or two have spent their labour, their wealth, and their lives in search of

Though earlier navigators may have reached the peninsula before him, Juan Ponce de León, of whom there is reliable evidence, is generally credited with being the discoverer of Florida. Juan Ponce served as governor of Puerto Rico, which he had conquered, from 1509 to 1512. On March 3, 1513, at thirty-nine years of age, he led a three-ship expedition northwest from that island in search of a fabled isle with equally fabled waters said to have rejuvenating powers. After sailing through the Bahama Islands, Juan Ponce stumbled upon a large landmass which he thought was an island and to which he gave the name La Florida *(the flowery land), "because it was very pretty to behold with many refreshing trees." The date was April 2. He anchored, went ashore to speak with the natives, and formally took possession of the "island." A recent resailing of Juan Ponce's route suggests that his landing site was at or near Melbourne Beach, south of Cape Canaveral.*

Would-be conquistador Hernando de Soto anchored in Tampa Bay in May 1539 with over 600 soldiers, 12 priests, two women, 223 horses, numerous mules and war dogs, and a herd of swine. Soon after landing, his men discovered a Spaniard named Juan Ortíz, a straggler from an earlier exploration, who had spent over a decade as a captive of the Florida natives. He would serve as an interpreter. De Soto's march through Florida in search of gold passed through the present localities of Dade City, Williston, Gainesville, Lake City, and Tallahassee. At Tallahassee the expedition passed the winter of 1539–40. (The encampment was discovered in 1987 scarcely a mile from the capitol and has since been excavated by archaeologists.) De Soto treated the native people he encountered there with unbecoming cruelty. Not surprisingly, they resisted him almost everywhere with bows and arrows and other weapons, as represented in this mural painted by Charles Hardman in the Miami Beach Post Office. Contagious diseases unwittingly left behind by the Spaniards continued to ravage the Florida populations long after de Soto marched into present-day Georgia, the Carolinas, Tennessee, Alabama, Mississippi, Arkansas, and beyond.

a golden kingdom without getting further notice of it than what they had at their first setting forth, all of which notwithstanding, the third, and fourth, and fifth undertakers have not been disheartened."

So it was in Florida over the space of fifty-odd years before the first successful settlement. Failure followed failure as a long succession of Spanish captains, beginning with Ponce de León, carried their proud lances into this wilderness only to see them broken by outrageous fortune. Here there was no sated conqueror resting amid Aztec splendor, no master of Inca wealth and magnificence. What we see instead is Ponce de León at Charlotte Harbor staggering from the native arrow that would carry off his life; Pánfilo de Narváez attempting escape from the coast below Tallahassee, his rough-hewn raft awash and the Gulf of

In 1564 a French expedition of three hundred men and four women, commanded by René Goulaine de Laudonnière, established a colony named Fort Caroline near the mouth of the St. Johns River, which the French called the River May. The fort was a direct challenge to Spain's claims over La Florida. A triangular-shaped wall of earth berms and logs with a moat, as shown in this drawing by Jacques Le Moyne, Fort Caroline was not fated to last long in French hands. Pedro Menéndez de Avilés, who founded St. Augustine nearby in 1565, captured the fort in the same year. Neither Fort Caroline nor an earlier colony of the Spaniards at Pensacola (1559–61) could claim to be the first (impermanent) European settlement in this country. That honor belonged to the short-lived Spanish colony of San Miguel de Gualdape at Sapelo Sound, Georgia, in 1526.

Mexico in his lungs; Hernando de Soto, the "never conquered cavalier," fruitlessly seeking gold through Florida's dense interior and dying three years away on the banks of the Mississippi; Dominican friar Luis Cáncer de Barbastro, slaughtered at Tampa Bay before he could do any more than hold aloft the crucifix before his native assassins; Tristán de Luna, a failure in the eyes of both his colonists and his viceroy after two inglorious years at Pensacola Bay.

Even Menéndez failed in most of his purposes. True, he founded a city and he accomplished his immediate military mission, the destruction of Fort Caroline, a French settlement established by René de Laudonnière at the mouth of the St. Johns River—an action that included the brutal slaying of French soldiers and sailors under Jean Ribault on the beaches south of St. Augustine. But he failed to find a son, Juan, lost at sea off La Florida in 1563; Florida soil never produced great crops under the Spanish hand; St. Augustine was of negligible importance as a protector of the Bahama Channel through which Spain sent its treasure fleets twice each year; and it would be difficult to describe the city as a military stronghold when, for a century and a half, a pirate who passed by could sack it with ease, as Francis Drake did in 1586 and Robert Searles in 1668. Following the Drake raid, Spain abandoned its exposed northern settlement of Santa Elena (Parris Island, South Carolina), which Menéndez had established to be the first capital of the provinces of Florida.

La Florida was not seen by Menéndez in the beginning as a battlefield. Its conquest and settlement were undertaken as a commercial enterprise. Menéndez, an entrepreneur, aspired to be Florida's first great land developer, industrialist, and agribusinessman. Before his death in 1574 some nine Spanish Asturian families, all closely related to the founder by blood and marriage, had joined with him to invest in the venture. Unhappily, their returns were meager. The reasons were many: no discoveries of precious metals, gems, or minerals; no abundant crops in the infertile coastal soil; the general ineffectiveness of Menéndez's native American ("Indian") policy; costly fraud by corrupt minor officials; and numerous mutinies by his troops.

Throughout most of its "first Spanish period" (1565–1763), Florida's European population had to depend on an economic subsidy, the *situado*, sent each year from Mexico City. This annual allowance of specie (cash), food, and supplies was sometimes pilfered or delayed. To supplement imported foods the Spaniards adopted the diet and food preparation techniques of the surrounding natives. Spanish plans to develop a colonial dyestuffs industry based on cochineal and indigo failed, as did efforts to smoke fish for export and to develop the culture of silkworms. Menéndez had not launched a thriving enterprise.

There were occasional successes. Franciscan missionaries

Pedro Menéndez de Avilés (1519–74), shown here in an engraving based on a painting, was the founder of Florida. It was Menéndez who on September 8, 1565, established Florida's and the country's first permanent European settlement. He gave it the name St. Augustine, because it was on that saint's feast day, August 28, when he had made his first Florida landfall (sighting), at Cape Canaveral. Arriving at the St. Augustine site with 500 soldiers, 200 sailors, and 100 others, Menéndez hastily fortified a site belonging to the Seloy tribe of the Timucuan nation. As expected, he was soon attacked by the French coming south by ship from Fort Caroline. A storm wrecked the French fleet, however, and Menéndez dealt mercilessly with the survivors. Reproduced from Cesaréo Fernández Duro, Armada España.

instructed the Apalachee Indians around present-day Tallahassee in the cultivation of maize, wheat, beans, pumpkins, tobacco, and cotton, the last two valuable trade crops. In some years when the *situado* was interrupted or war threatened, the fertile hills of Apalachee became an emergency breadbasket. A more permanently successful agriculture might have developed in the region if the sometimes oppressive policies of the governors toward the natives had been more accommodating. In the Alachua prairie, near present-day Gainesville, a thriving cattle industry developed in the seventeenth century. Cattle were driven from La Chua (Alachua), crossing the St. Johns by flatboat, to St. Augustine, where the fresh meat was sold for local consumption and the hides were tanned for shipment overseas. Some cattle, however, were smuggled to Cuba by way of the Suwannee River, thus avoiding export duties. In the first half of the eighteenth century the cattle ranches in Alachua collapsed under pressures from English and Indian rustlers. By 1763 the interior ranch lands were untended domains of buffalo, deer, wild black cattle, and ungoverned human runaways—natives, blacks, Englishmen, and others.

Of all the motives that led Menéndez to Florida, the only one that succeeded, besides the survival of his city, was the Christianization of the indigenous inhabitants. These first residents of Florida were remarkable peoples of rich and diverse cultures. It would be a mistake to think of them as "savages." Still, the Spaniards believed that Spain possessed a higher culture and a superior religion, which they felt compelled to impart to the Indians. Thus began the Florida missions, 204 years before Fray Junípero Serra's friars planted the first of a chain of missions in Alta California.

Missions

The first mission, Nombre de Dios ("Name of God"), was founded at St. Augustine by the secular priests who accompanied Menéndez in 1565. Jesuit missionaries came to the peninsula the next year, but their work was not successful. It was the Franciscans, arriving first in 1573, who eventually succeeded in building an effective mission system. By the middle of the next century they could count thirty-one missions in the peninsula (and five more to the north along the Georgia coastal islands). Altogether some 26,000 Christian Indians who lived in and around the missions were learning not only the catechism of the Roman Catholic faith but also the rudiments of European arts and crafts.

The Christianization and Europeanization of these native inhabitants were remarkable accomplishments for the missionaries, even if, in the long run, they succeeded in applying only a thin veneer of Christianity and Western culture over persistent aboriginal customs and beliefs. Mission documents of the period express that worry again and again. Still, the Franciscan friars must be credited with unusual dedication, to their God and to the people whom they served. The records only hint at the hardships voluntarily undertaken by these men in order to administer sacraments in the wilderness: the constant hunger, tribal warfare, long and exhausting overland treks, sweltering days, and mosquito-filled nights. Theirs were truly committed lives, devoid of ambition for human glory or pleasure. One of them, Fray Francisco Pareja, justly stated, "We are the ones who bear the burden and the heat." Of them may be said what historian Francis Parkman wrote of Jesuit missionaries later in Canada: "Men steeped in antique learning, pale with the close breath of the cloister, here spent the noon and evening of their lives . . . and stood serene before the direst shapes of death."

The missionaries appear to have had no other purpose than to elevate the minds and spirits of the Indians among whom they dwelled. They did not expropriate their lands or push them back along an ever-advancing frontier, as happened later with the Indian lands of the Anglo-American country to the north. To thousands of Indians the missionaries taught European farming, cattle raising, carpentry, weaving, and, in many instances, reading and writing. Theirs was a heroic humanitarian effort for the amelioration and spiritual development of Florida's indigenous peoples, though it must be noted that the record was not uniformly inspiring: toward the end of the seventeenth century many of the friars were being described by members of their own order as lacking in the original Franciscan spirit, as though a kind of Florida weariness had overcome them.

Lacking proper tools for quarrying Florida's rock formations underground, the Franciscan friars and their Indian converts built the Florida mission buildings from wood or from wattle and daub. Here, in an artist's reconstruction, wattles (latticework) between upright poles are covered with daub (clay). In 1674–75 the missions were visited by Gabriel Díaz Vara Calderón, Bishop of Santiago de Cuba. In a report to Queen Mariana dated in the latter year, the bishop gave an illuminating picture of the missions, together with measurements of the distances that lay between them. With the help of Calderón, archaeologists have been able to locate the foundations of nearly half of the mission sites named in his report. Calderón states that the mission Indians were "clever and quick to learn any art they see done, and great carpenters as is evidenced in the construction of their wooden churches which are large and painstakingly wrought."

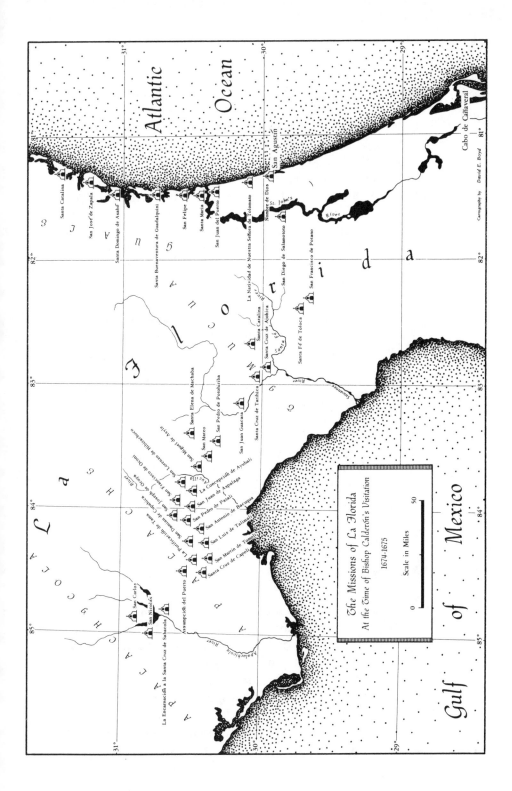

The Missions of La Florida
At the Time of Bishop Calderón's Visitation
1674-1675

Scale in Miles
0   50

Cartography by   David E. Boyd

Atlantic   Ocean

Gulf   of   Mexico

Cabo de Cañaveral

F l o r i d a

A p a l a c h e e

C H A C A T O

G U A L E

T I M U C U A

Santa Catalina
San José de Zapala
Santa Domingo de Asaho
Santa Buenaventura de Guadalquini
San Felipe
Santa María
San Juan del Puerto
La Natividad de Nuestra Señora de Tolomato
Nombre de Dios
San Agustín
San Diego de Salamototo
San Francisco de Potano
Santa Cruz de Ajohica
Santa Fé de Toloca
Santa Catalina
San Juan Guacara
Santa Cruz de Tarihica
San Pedro de Potohiriba
Santa Elena de Machaba
San Mateo
San Miguel de Asyle
San Lorenzo de Hitauhuco
San Francisco de Oconi
San Joseph de Ocuya
San Juan de Aspalaga
La Concepción de Ayubali
San Pedro de Patali
San Damian de Cupaica
La Purificación de Tama
San Antonio de Bacuqua
San Luis de Talimali
San Martin de Tomoli
Santa Cruz de Capoli
Assumpción del Puerto
La Encarnación a la Santa Cruz de Sabacola
San Nicolás
San Carlos

St. John's River
Santa Fé River
Suwannee River
Apalachicola River

81°
82°
83°
84°
85°

31°
30°
29°

The missions' end was tragic. In 1702, English governor James Moore of South Carolina led a raiding party that left the coastal missions in ruins. In 1704, he returned with Yamassee Indians and Carolina ruffians to destroy the missions in Apalachee. Most of the mission compounds he burned to the ground or depopulated; the few that survived, together with the Timucua missions, would be ravaged by other raiding parties in succeeding years. Three Franciscans died defending their charges in Apalachee, as did many of the mission Indians: some the English and Yamassees impaled on stakes, others they burned slowly until, mercifully, death delivered them. Those Christian Indians who escaped Moore's marauders fled in terror to the woods. Some went to St. Augustine; some were reported to have gone as far west as Mobile. By his own estimate, Moore took several thousand captives whom he sold into slavery or settled in villages among the Yamassee. A great civilizing work of the human spirit was wrecked. Only in the last half century, thanks to research undertaken by Florida historians and archaeologists, has the veil drawn over that gratuitous massacre by English-oriented writers of our national history been lifted from the frontier proscenium. The missions would never again achieve their former extent or influence. After Florida was ceded to the English in 1763, they would disappear altogether—and with them many of the last survivors of the original Indian societies, taking into oblivion the oral traditions that were the only form in which their histories had been preserved.

Military and Civil Life

At the end of the seventeenth century, Spain established two political and military monuments that last to this day. The first was the town of Pensacola, founded for the second time, and permanently, in 1698. With its wooden Fort San Carlos de Austria, Pensacola would attempt to guard the western approaches to Florida against French incursions from the Mississippi Valley and the Gulf of Mexico. The deep water port would play a major role throughout Florida's colonial history, though various flags successively

The Castillo de San Marcos (Castle of St. Mark) at St. Augustine. Begun in 1672 and substantially completed twenty-three years later, it was constructed entirely from slabs of shellrock called coquina *quarried on Anastasia Island across the river from the site. Coquina consists of tiny mollusk shells cemented together by their own lime. (A visitor to the Castillo can easily discern the individual shells in a slab.) The shellrock, which is unique to four coastal sites worldwide, three in Florida, had an unexpected city-saving property: When the British bombarded the castle in 1702 and 1704, the coquina walls, rather than shattering from the impact, simply absorbed the cannonballs. At the end of the two sieges the intact castle looked like a chocolate chip cookie.*

went up and down the masts of its presidios: Spanish, French, Spanish, French, Spanish, English, Spanish, English, U.S., Spanish, U.S., and Spanish once again. Because of the great distance separating them, Spanish Pensacola and St. Augustine would have closer contacts with Havana than they would have with each other.

The second monument was the extraordinary fortress Castillo de San Marcos (Castle of St. Mark), built at St. Augustine and substantially completed, after twenty-three years of labor, in 1695. It replaced nine successive wooden forts. Built entirely of *coquina*, a native shellrock, the fortress twice repulsed massive sieges by the English, the first by Colonel James Moore of Carolina in 1702, when the entire city was put to the torch, and the second by Governor James Edward Oglethorpe of Georgia in 1740. San Marcos was one of the military bases intended by Spain to string a cordon of fire from Panama to Colombia, Cuba, Puerto Rico, and Florida. It stands today, its dank gray walls brooding over the city it saved. Not to be overlooked are the nearby remains of Fort Mose, begun in 1738, the first free African-American fort and town in the continent.

The governmental structure of Spanish Florida was never complex in theory, since almost total authority in the province was held by the governor. The only other royally appointed officials were the sergeant major and captains of the military garrison and the officials of the royal treasury. Each function of government was authorized by the king operating through his Council of the Indies. Regional superintendence of the Florida provinces was given to the viceroy of Mexico and the governor-general of Cuba, neither of whom relished the responsibility since unproductive Florida was a continual drain on their treasuries. Minor officials in the colony were frequently the products of royal favoritism or the selling of offices; many were guaranteed their offices for life and tended to form an entrenched, even hereditary, bureaucracy. The more venal among them were guilty of such offenses as misappropriation of funds, illicit trade, absenteeism, slipshod judicial practices, and careless accounting. Toward these failings the king and his council were generally indulgent, tolerating in the hardship post of Florida practices that would have brought harsh punishment in Mexico or Peru. When necessary, the governor would form a temporary advisory council, or *junta*, composed of the military commander, treasury officials, and pastor of the principal church, and frequently other Spanish governmental institutions were found at St. Augustine, such as a town council, or *cabildo*, familiar elsewhere in the Spanish Americas.

The native peoples, who had forty towns to the Spaniards' one, lived throughout the seventeenth century in a relatively autonomous society that the Spaniards called the "Republic of Indians." Occupying different regions of the same *La Florida*, the natives paid no head tax to the "Republic of Spaniards," nor, unlike their counterparts in Mexico or Peru, were they required to labor in mines or workhouses; they did, however, have to pay tribute of goods and labor to the garrison at St. Augustine. The Florida Indians enjoyed rights to inherit titles and offices, to own land and rule vassals, and, in the case of chiefs and nobles, to wear swords and go about on horseback. They were protected from molestation by rules that forbade any Spaniard on legitimate business among them from staying longer than three days in an Indian town (where the visitor also was constricted to sleeping in the official building, the council house). Only the Franciscan friars, considered members of the Indian societies, were exempted from this rule. When addressing the native peoples the Spanish governors used the expression "my sons and cousins." That general familiarity and respect did not, however, prevent several of the governors in the century from exploiting Indian nobles as *cargadores* to carry food supplies, mule-like, on their backs from the deep interior to St. Augustine—a practice stopped in one notable instance by a vigorous defense of the nobles' rights made by the friars over the head of the governor to the king.

Eventually Spain would have to yield on paper what it had never yielded on the field of battle. To the north France and England were contending for hegemony over the larger part of the continent: French fur-hunting ranges were pushing eastward from the Mississippi and the Great Lakes while English farmsteads were moving westward from the Atlantic. In the inevitable collision, which we call the French and Indian War (1754–63), Spain, worried about English dominance over the continent, threw in its lot with France in 1761. It was a disastrous decision, for England quickly and easily seized Havana. In the humiliating peace treaty that followed, Spain had to sacrifice Florida in order to regain the rich Cuban port. France lost much more—all of its North American territories, including Canada. Louisiana might have been kept but instead was given in gratitude to Spain. Florida was now English, and the treaty provisions placed the western boundary of Florida at the Mississippi River.

Following two captures of its fort by the French in 1719, and two recoveries, the last in 1822, the Spanish colony at Pensacola moved from the mainland to Santa Rosa Island across the bay. Here, artist Dominic Serres depicts the Presidio Isla de Santa Rosa as it appeared in 1743. The fort is shown at the far left. Moving to the right: the Commandant's house, a well, the church, and the governor's house (to the right of the church). The position of the garrison and settlement was always precarious. Fires were a constant problem. The settlers had little success growing crops in the light, sandy soil. Cattle and sheep were imported but did not prosper. At one point the population dwindled to about eighty-five. In 1747, the colony had to buy off threatening Uchize Indians with half its meager supplies. In 1752 a hurricane forced removal of the settlement back to the mainland, where Pensacola has since remained.

Two Decades of British Rule

Florida was so extensive from east to west, in fact, that Britain created out of it two separate colonies: East Florida, with a capital at St. Augustine, and West Florida, with a capital at Pensacola. The Apalachicola River became the boundary between them. About these fourteenth and fifteenth North American English colonies little is said in the history books, because in the American Revolution they would remain loyal to the British crown.

The first civil governor of West Florida, George Johnstone, arrived in Pensacola in October 1764. He found an excellent harbor and an impressive military structure but little else. Five British governors would preside over West Florida between 1764 and 1783. At the transfer of power in

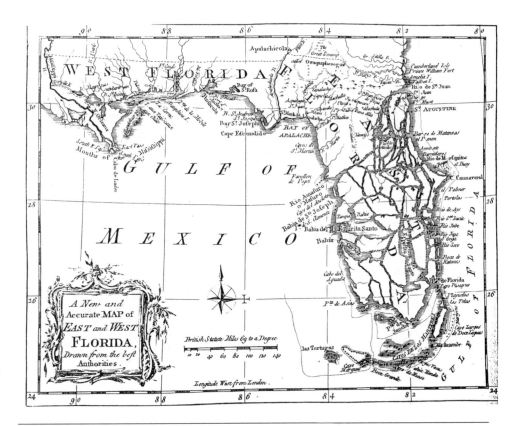

This map of British origin dates from 1763, when Spanish Florida became two British colonies, East and West Florida, divided at the Apalachicola River. "Drawn from the best Authorities," it is, for its time, quite an accurate representation of the peninsula and Panhandle except that the cartographer greatly exaggerated the size of Florida's rivers and bays. Though San Agustín has become St. Augustine (the English form), most of the original Spanish geographic names have been retained here, e.g., Laguna del Espiritu Santo (Lake of the Holy Spirit) for Lake Okeechobee and R[ío] S[an] Martín for the Suwannee. The Quaker naturalist William Bartram in 1774 described the Suwannee as "the cleanest and purest of any river" he had ever seen, "almost as transparent as the air we breathe."

East Florida, the entire Spanish population of 3,046 persons took ship, most for Cuba. The first British governor, James Grant from Scotland, arrived at St. Augustine in August 1764 and took office in the old Spanish governor's residence. From there he and his two successors could look out on a shady plaza that ran to a guardhouse on the bay, on small coquina houses with overhanging balconies, and on a bustling population that for many years would labor as fruitlessly to draw wealth from Florida's coastal resources as the Spaniards had done before them.

The acquisition of the Floridas was very much to Britain's advantage. The colonies rounded out her possessions from Canada to the Mississippi; the Spanish haven for runaway black slaves from Georgia and the Carolinas was closed; an entry could be made into the rich southern fur trade begun by France; and although it was not known at the time, England would have in the Floridas two loyal refuges for Tories during the American Revolution. Numerous visitors from English colonies to the north touted the Floridas for their natural beauty and abundance of plant and animal species. Notable was the thirty-five-year-old Quaker naturalist from Philadelphia, William Bartram, who toured the region in 1774 and published a glowing account of his travels that became an inspiration for later Romantic poets such as Wordsworth and Coleridge.

In West Florida the principal products were furs, barrel staves, and naval stores. Some agriculture was carried on around the old French settlements of Mobile, Biloxi, Natchez, and Baton Rouge. In East Florida the economy turned principally on agriculture. Vast tracts of land were cleared along the St. Johns River and the seacoast, and, aside from St. Augustine, the plantations were the centers of life in the colony. The most elegant of the country homes, Governor John Moultrie's "Bella Vista," stood on the Matanzas River. Surrounding the ten-room stone mansion were parkland, formal gardens, walkways, fish ponds, and a bowling green. An Englishman could close his eyes and imagine, in the distance, the baying of foxhounds. (Bella Vista was destroyed by Indians following the departure of the British.) The chief crops on the plantations were indigo and rice. Oranges, which had been introduced by the Spaniards, were grown and exported, as was timber. The most famous of the plantations was that of Andrew Turnbull, a Scottish physician, at New Smyrna, which Turnbull named after the birthplace of his Greek wife. Turnbull brought 300 families to New Smyrna from the British-held Mediterranean island of Minorca, together with other colonists from Greece and Italy. They came as indentured servants. It was, reported Governor Grant, "the largest importation of white inhabitants that was ever brought into America at a time." The indigo plantation was a failure, however, and the colonists, after nine years of sickness and death, protests and punish-

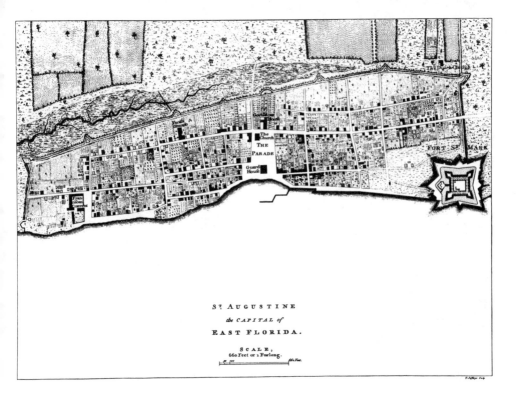

S. AUGUSTINE
the CAPITAL *of*
EAST FLORIDA.

SCALE,
660 Feet or 1 Furlong.

This plan of St. Augustine by Thomas Jefferys shows the appearance of the old Spanish city and fort (castillo) after their occupation by Britain in 1763. Despite the changes in street and places-names to English—for example, the central plaza became The Parade—the city maintained its Spanish character throughout the twenty-one-year interregnum. Church of England authorities added a steeple to the Catholic parish church (on Calle Real, renamed St. George Street) and renamed it St. Peter's. Two-story coquina and wood houses with overhanging balconies lined the narrow streets. The streets all exist today. Most houses had backyard vegetable gardens and fruit trees—oranges, grapefruit, lemon, peach, pomegranate, fig, and quince. The María Sánchez Creek, beyond the city wall, formed the western boundary of the narrow city.

ment, fled to safety in St. Augustine, where many of the Minorcan names can be found today.

Florida had a variegated population during the British period. Many English migrated from the north. One, who stayed awhile and purchased a home and lot in Pensacola, was Daniel Boone. Most numerous were blacks, of whom the great majority were slaves. Not only did they till the fields and operate the mills; they also sailed as crew members of naval and merchant ships, where frequently they outnumbered whites. In the last few decades before the

The Spanish Governor's House at St. Augustine, painted by an English artist in 1764. On the city's central plaza, with a view of the Matanzas River beyond, this structure succeeded other governors' residences on the site, including a coquina and wood house that was burned by the British under Colonel James Moore following their failed siege of the city in 1702. The house was restored in 1713 and further improved in 1759. When the British took over the Floridas in 1763, they imported skilled laborers from Charleston to install window glass and make necessary repairs. Provided with ample rum rations, the workers must have missed the roof. The third British governor, Patrick Tonyn, arriving to take up residence eleven years later, declared that the roof was like a sieve: "I have been drove out of every room by the rain." Much modified, parts of the colonial building stand today—sheltered by a sound roof.

Spanish departure, Creek Indians from the districts of the Chattahoochee and Flint rivers in present-day Georgia and Alabama had moved south to Alachua and other areas in Florida where the scattered Christian tribes had previously lived. The British called them "Seminoles" after the Creek word for "wild ones" or "separatists." Governor Grant won praise for the successful treaties he struck with them. In the towns a visitor could find, alongside proper officials and merchants, large numbers of unruly soldiers and sailors, and alongside bathhouses and bookstores, bawdy houses and taverns. A great many languages were heard: English (often with a Scottish burr), Mandingo, Muskogee, Hitchiti,

James Grant, from Scotland, was the first civil governor of East Florida during the British period, serving from 1764 to 1771. He had spent considerable time in the American colonies as a military officer, seeing action against the French and their Indian allies in Canada and the Ohio country, as well as against the Cherokees in South Carolina. During his administration, St. Augustine was a disorderly garrison town, where, as one visitor commented, "Luxury and debauchery reigned amidst scarcity and the small number of females occasioned much division and irregularity." That appeared to be fine with Grant. He wrote to a friend in Scotland, "There is not so gay a Town in America as this is at present, the People [are] Musick and Dancing mad." During Grant's first year in office he and his houseguests consumed 236 gallons of rum, 216 gallons of wine, 1,200 bottles of claret, and 519 bottles of port. In May 1771 Grant sailed home to England, thoroughly pickled and gouty.

Cherokee, Catalan, Greek, French, German, Spanish, Italian, and Sicilian.

The effect of the revolutionary war on East Florida was pronounced though indirect. With the major fighting far away and tax monies plentifully supplied by Parliament, Floridians remained loyal to King George III. Thousands of Tory refugees from Savannah, Charleston, and other seaboard points poured into St. Augustine or settled along the St. Johns, swelling the colony's population from 6,000 persons to over 17,000 at the war's end. The more talented newcomers produced plays and books and published Florida's first newspaper, the *East Florida Gazette*. Numerous patriot leaders also came to St. Augustine, as prisoners, including three signers of the Declaration of Independence: Arthur Middleton, Thomas Heyward, Jr., and Edward Rutledge.

Although about a tenth of the British army was stationed in the Floridas, the military forces in East Florida did little fighting. Defending the St. Marys border from patriot forays out of Georgia was their principal activity. The southernmost incursion of the patriots, in 1778, was repulsed at Alligator Creek bridge at the headwaters of the Nassau River. In West Florida, British military activity was more intense but less successful. Spain entered the war on the patriot side in June 1779, and the governor of Spanish Louisiana, Bernardo de Gálvez, quickly struck at British forces guarding Baton Rouge, Mobile, and Pensacola. The seizure of Pensacola in May 1781 came at the end of the largest battle ever fought in Florida. By that year, Spain had recaptured all of West Florida. In the treaty ending the Revolution two years later (1783), East Florida was also returned to Spain.

The Second Spanish Period

Spain's second occupancy of Florida was tenuous at best. From the beginning it was clear that Florida could not long withstand the expansionist ambitions of the infant United States of America. Whereas Spain had earlier attempted to

During the British period West Florida stretched from the Apalachicola River westward as far as the Mississippi. Its capital was Pensacola. Other notable communities in the colony, now parts of Alabama, Louisiana, and Mississippi, included Mobile, Baton Rouge, and Natchez. When Spain came into the American Revolution on the side of the patriots in June 1779, the courageous twenty-seven-year-old Spanish governor of Louisiana, Bernardo de Gálvez, moved at once to seize Baton Rouge, Natchez, and three other British forts in the Mississippi Valley. With reinforcements from Cuba, he captured Mobile in March 1780 and, after two months of heavy fighting, forced the surrender of Pensacola in May 1781, completing the seizure of all of West Florida. In the last action, where he was wounded, he sailed virtually alone into Pensacola Bay to give inspiration to his men. In recognition of that deed, the King of Spain awarded him a coat of arms depicting a ship with the motto Yo solo—"I alone."

pacify and control the interior through its line of missions (an attempt defeated by the Moore raids), in this second possession it intended to hold the Floridas by trade and immigration. The resulting prosperity, it was hoped, would cause Floridians from the Atlantic to the Mississippi to resist both blandishments and threats from the new nation. To promote trade Spain gave special standing and privileges to an English company, Panton, Leslie and Company, a holdover from the British occupation. Indian alliances originally forged by the British, particularly that with Alexander McGillivray, half-breed chieftain of the Creek nation, were continued. This part of Spain's two-pronged policy proved successful, except that for a time (1788–1802) Spanish control over Indian trade was sorely tested by an English freebooter out of the Bahamas, William Augustus Bowles. With the support of Seminole and Lower Creek Indians, Bowles interrupted Spanish commerce on both land and sea, even successfully besieging the Spanish fort in Apalachee, and declared an independent nation of "Muscogee." Captured, he died a prisoner at Havana in 1805.

The other half of Spain's policy, immigration, proved Spain's undoing in West Florida. The more that land grants were made available, the more Anglo-Americans poured in from the north; and the more local populations became non-Spanish, the more the province became independence-minded. U.S. Secretary of State Thomas Jefferson wrote to President George Washington in 1791: "I wish 10,000 of our inhabitants would accept the invitation. It would be the means of delivering to us peaceably what must otherwise cost us a war. In the meantime, we may complain of the seduction of our inhabitants just enough to make the Spanish believe it is a very wise policy for them." The inevitable happened: In 1810 the Anglo-Americans in Baton Rouge established a government of their own and declared themselves the "Republic of West Florida." President James Madison seized on the event by annexing the lands between the Mississippi and Pearl rivers; in 1813 the United States annexed the remaining lands of West Florida as far as the Perdido River, the present western boundary of the state of Florida.

In East Florida, meanwhile, there were several independent governments founded by adventurers in and around the town of Fernandina on Amelia Island, where in the last years of Spanish rule one could see the flags of the declared "Green Cross Republic" or the "Republic of Mexico." One of the more colorful claimants was Gregor McGregor, an English soldier-of-fortune who had fought in the Napoleonic Wars. American agents, acting under ill-defined instructions from Washington, were taking advantage of the instability in the province and Spain's inability to defend it. The clearest indications of Spain's weakness came in the War of 1812 and in the First Seminole War.

With the outbreak of war between the United States and Great Britain, British forces seized Pensacola to use as a Gulf Coast base and began to stir up trouble with the Creek Indians. Indian fighter General Andrew Jackson and his Tennessee troops descended on the Creek nation, forced the surrender of the British-held fortifications at Pensacola, and then pushed on to spectacular victory over the British at New Orleans. Both British and U.S. forces had moved with impunity through Spanish-claimed Florida. Jackson would return to do the same in 1818, leading a punitive expedition against rebellious Seminole tribes. Seizing the Spanish fort of St. Marks (below Tallahassee), the new national hero quickly put down the rebellion, executed two British traders whom he accused of fomenting the uprisings, and, for good measure, marched on Pensacola, where he brashly, and successfully, demanded the surrender of the Spanish forts.

The United States Acquires Florida

Spain had no alternative but to get out of Florida under the best terms it could secure. To that end, on February 22, 1819, its minister to the United States, Don Luis de Onís, and Secretary of State John Quincy Adams signed a treaty of cession by which, in return for Florida, the United States assumed $5 million worth of Spanish debts to American citizens. Other provisions of the treaty required the United States to surrender any claims to Texas. The Senate ratified the treaty two days later, and Spain, after internal political changes, did so two years later. Andrew Jackson thereupon made his third trip to Florida, this time as the first military governor of the new U.S. possession. Impressive ceremonies including the exchange of flags took place at Pensacola and St. Augustine in the summer of 1821.

Jackson resigned after three months to return to Tennessee but not before he issued ordinances and established precedents that would begin the Americanization of Florida. Among his actions were the division of Florida into two counties, Escambia and St. Johns, provision for trial by jury, and establishment of county courts. The possession formally became the Territory of Florida on March 4, 1822, and in the same month Congress provided for a tripartite territorial government with the usual executive, legislative, and judicial branches. The first territorial governor, William P. Duval, was appointed in May of the same year. A native of Virginia, he had spent most of his life in Kentucky. He would remain in office for four terms, until 1834.

Territorial Years and Statehood

The first session of Florida's Legislative Council met on July 22, 1822, at Pensacola. The members from St. Augustine had traveled fifty-nine days by water to attend. One result of the first session was the formation of two new counties, Duval (out of St. Johns) and Jackson (out of Escambia). The second legislative session met at St. Augustine in the following year. This time it was the western delegates who had been inconvenienced: shipwrecked in the passage around the peninsula, they had barely escaped death. Not surprisingly, the principal decision made at the second session was to select a halfway location for a capital

This engraving of Andrew Jackson (1767–1845) was based on a painting for which Jackson sat in 1815. After brief careers as U.S. congressman and senator from Tennessee, and superior court judge, Jackson embarked on a military career, leading Tennessee troops to victories in the War of 1812, where he became the national hero "Old Hickory," and in the First Seminole War of 1818. After Florida became a possession of the United States in 1821, Jackson reentered Florida as military governor. Known for his abrupt and cavalier behavior, Jackson was true to form during his brief three-month stay in that capacity. He clashed repeatedly with the outgoing Spanish governor at Pensacola, José Callava, over change-of-flag details, at one point clapping the Spaniard in jail. In short order he succeeded in Americanizing the new possession. Jacksonville, a site he never visited, is named for him.

that would shorten the sea voyage and the twenty-eight-day overland crossing from St. Augustine to Pensacola.

Two appointed commissioners selected the Indian fields of Tallahassee in the old Apalachee land, now occupied by the Creeks. Congress approved the site as the capital, and the third legislative session, in 1824, met there in a rude log capitol, where Indians leaned through the windows to hear the strange goings-on. A stone building would be started two years later. Among the decisions in 1824 were laws to establish ferries over rivers, to incorporate churches and towns, and to authorize construction of roads, highways, and canals.

Florida's population of 1821 numbered fewer than 8,000 persons, including black slaves, but it grew rapidly from immigration, particularly in the cotton lands of "middle Florida." There, by the 1830s, the counties of Jackson, Gadsden, Leon, Jefferson, and Madison had not only half the territorial population of 34,530 persons (the majority of them black slaves) but also the majority of the territory's wealth and culture. For productivity the region's cotton plantations rivaled those in the adjoining states, though there were few examples on the Florida landscape of "Gone with the Wind" mansions and planter aristocracy. Most owners worked the fields alongside their slaves. One of the most important plantations of the period was established by Scotland-born Zephaniah Kingsley and his African wife, Anna Jai, seventeen miles northeast of Jacksonville.

There were certain boom towns, too, notably Apalachicola and St. Joseph, twenty-two miles apart, which profited from their positions as Gulf ports for up-country river commerce. A yellow fever epidemic, followed soon afterward by a hurricane, destroyed St. Joseph in 1841. Pensacola grew erratically, a brief boom period shortened by yellow fever. Lumber and naval stores were its principal industries. The city was linked to St. Augustine in 1826 by the "military road," constructed across the Panhandle under the direction of U.S. Quartermaster Corps Captain Daniel E. Burch, and its extension eastward from Tallahassee, called the "Bellamy Road" after a rich planter, John Bellamy, who built a great part of it.

St. Augustine remained the most important city on the east coast. Until 1835, when a prolonged freeze killed all the trees, it was the center of the citrus industry. Jacksonville, called Cowford in British times because of the shallowness of the St. Johns there, was renamed to honor General Andrew Jackson. The first streets were laid out in 1822. Jacksonville stood alongside the first major road in Florida,

Tallahassee was a compromise selection as the state's capital after Florida became a U.S. territory. The principal point in its favor was that it stood midway between the two major population centers, St. Augustine and Pensacola. Another was that it was relatively free of yellow fever that afflicted the seaport towns. The first meeting of the Legislative Council at Tallahassee in 1824 took place in a rude log hut. In 1826 the cornerstone was laid for a permanent statehouse, shown here. The brick structure measured thirty by twenty-four feet on a side. The council occupied the upper story, the executive and judicial branches the lower. A larger capitol, which became the core of the capitol building that served until 1978, was erected in 1839.

called King's Road, which the British had built to unite New Smyrna in the south with St. Marys on the Georgia border. Once prominent, Fernandina declined in population and importance. Numerous new towns sprang up in the 1820s and 1830s, among them Mayport, Green Cove Springs, Palatka—like Jacksonville a "cow ford"—Alachua, Micanopy, Ocala, and Tampa. South of the headwaters of the St. Johns River there were no settlements of note until one reached Key West, where a U.S. naval station was established and a flourishing salvage industry made it one of the important early towns in Florida.

Two problems vexed Florida's government during territorial days: Spanish land grants and the Seminole Indians. Certain large tracts of interior lands granted by the Spanish monarch to individuals prior to American occupation were in litigation for years during the territorial period. Among these were the Forbes grant of 1.3 million acres on the lower Apalachicola River and the Arredondo grant of 289,600 acres in the Alachua district. More serious were the Indian grants legitimized in a treaty negotiated in 1823 with leaders of the Seminole nation by representatives of the territorial and federal governments. Over four hundred Indians attended the treaty negotiations at Moultrie Creek, five miles south of St. Augustine, where the chiefs agreed to remove their people to a protected reservation of 4 million acres north of Charlotte Harbor and south of Ocala but not within twenty miles of either coast. In the years immediately following, the treaty proved unsatisfactory to both Indians and whites. The chiefs complained that the designated lands were too small to support their peoples; the whites, lusting after the rich interior farmlands, proposed a policy of general Indian removal to the trans-Mississippi West. That policy took formal shape at Payne's Landing on the Ocklawaha River in 1832, where seven chiefs and eight subchiefs (compared to thirty-two signers at Moultrie Creek) signed a treaty pledging that they would move to Arkansas, provided seven of their number inspected the new lands and approved of them. A delegation duly visited the western lands and signed a ratifying document at Fort Gibson, Arkansas. The federal government made plans for Indian removal within three years, but a number of Seminole chiefs rejected the treaty.

On December 28, 1835, Indians shot and killed an Indian agent and a lieutenant outside Fort King, near Ocala. On the same day Indians ambushed Major Francis L. Dade and two companies of soldiers, of whom only three survived, near Bushnell. Thus began the Second Seminole War, the longest and most expensive Indian war in the country's history. For nearly seven years, in a guerrilla campaign unlike any that the U.S. Army had fought before, the Seminoles resisted a massive military effort to drive them from their homes.

The Seminole Indian chief Osceola, of popular lore, was neither Seminole nor chief. Born Billy Powell, or Osceola, to an English father and Upper Creek Indian mother in Alabama about 1804, he moved with his mother to Florida shortly before the Second Seminole War broke out. During three years of that conflict, he fought for the Seminole cause, becoming a war leader of ruthless daring. In 1837 he was captured during a parley under a white flag of truce by forces under U.S. Major General Thomas S. Jesup, a treacherous action that caused widespread public revulsion and made Osceola a martyr and legend. Here, a prisoner, and a short time before his death in 1838, he is depicted by artist George Catlin, who called him "an extraordinary character."

No lighthouse, of the thirty-one that dot Florida's 1,300–linear mile coastline, has had a more dramatic history than the ninety-five-foot high Cape Florida light at the southeastern tip of Key Biscayne (near Miami). Only sixty-five feet in height when first built in 1825, the brick tower was besieged by Seminole Indians eleven years later during the Second Seminole War. When the Indians set fire to the wooden door, which ignited an interior oil tank, assistant lighthouse keeper John Thompson and a helper named Henry climbed to the top with a musket and a keg of gunpowder. The fire forced the men onto the outside platform at the top, where Henry was killed by gunshot. Thompson, choosing suicide, threw the powder keg down the shaft into the fire. The explosion did not kill him, but it was heard twelve miles away by a U.S. Navy ship, which sailed to the site and rescued the beleaguered keeper.

This view of Apalachicola, dated 1837, shows the city at the height of its boom period. Though its harbor was not the equal of Pensacola's, Apalachicola prospered from goods shipped down the deep navigable river that carried the same name. On the Gulf only Mobile and New Orleans had more commerce, trade, or population. Not everyone was pleased with the boom, which led to excesses and vice. A Methodist circuit rider ventured into the city once a month in an attempt to remedy its wickedness. On one occasion, he recorded that the hotel charged him and his horse the outrageous fee of $6.50 a night, that the desk clerk was drunk, and that the cursing and disorder in the other rooms was so loud he couldn't sleep. Giving up, he sought and received a kinder, gentler circuit.

Leading the U.S. forces were officers who would later distinguish themselves in the war with Mexico and in the Civil War. It would be hard to say that any, with the possible exception of Zachary Taylor, distinguished themselves against the Seminoles. The more durable heroes that emerged from the protracted agony were the chiefs and war leaders of the tribes, among them Osceola, Micanopy, Jumper, Alligator, Tiger Tail, and Coacoochee, who fought nobly against overwhelming odds. By 1834 a total of 3,824 Indians had been shipped westward. An uncaptured remnant took up arms against the white invaders during the 1850s in what is called the Third Seminole War. At its conclusion the survivors, fewer than one hundred in number, fled into the vastness of the Everglades, ending at last one of the darkest chapters in Florida's history.

Richard Keith Call was third (1836–39) and fifth (1841–44) civil governor of territorial Florida. Virginia-born, he fought as an officer under Andrew Jackson in the War of 1812 and the First Seminole War, earning the latter's lifelong esteem. He moved to Pensacola and was practicing law in that city when, in 1823, he was both promoted to brigadier general of the West Florida militia and elected territorial delegate to Congress. With his new wife, Mary Letitia Kirkman of Nashville, he moved to Tallahassee in 1825. In 1836 he was appointed to his first term as governor but had to give up his military commission, a decision by authorities in Washington that greatly embittered him. A strong Unionist as governor and afterward, he opposed secession when it came, stating that the rebel government had "opened the gates of Hell."

Following Duval were territorial governors John H. Eaton (1834–36), Richard Keith Call (who served two non-consecutive terms, 1836–39 and 1841–44), Robert Raymond Reid (1839–41), and John Branch (1844–45). In addition to subjugating the Indians and encouraging the economic development of the territory, the governors promoted statehood. East Florida, remembering the British and Spanish model of two provinces, was pushing for the establishment of two states; middle Florida wanted one state; and West Florida talked of annexation to Alabama.

The first significant step taken to resolve the issue was the convocation of a territorial constitutional convention at St. Joseph in 1838. A census taken that year listed a population of 48,223 persons, of whom 21,132 were slaves and 958 were free blacks. Although the total was 8,000 fewer than the number required for statehood, the convention, choosing one state over two, boldly drafted a constitution and submitted it to the people, who ratified it by a close vote.

The General Assembly, as the territorial legislature was now called, petitioned Congress for admission as a state. But it was not until 1845 that Congress finally passed a bill for admission, thanks to adroit lobbying by Florida's territorial delegate in Congress, David Levy (Yulee), and the support of Governor Branch. The bill was signed by President John Tyler on March 3 of that year, and Florida became the twenty-seventh state of the American Union. The practice of the time was to balance admission of slave and free states in order to keep the number of votes in the Senate equal; accordingly, the admission of Florida was balanced by the admission of Iowa in 1846. In the elections for offices, William D. Moseley, Jefferson County planter and Whig, became the state's first governor in a closely fought contest with Democrat Richard Keith Call. The first senators were James D. Westcott, Jr., and David Levy Yulee. The latter, who had changed his surname to his family's honorary Moorish title of *yulee*, became the first Jew in the country's history to hold the office of U.S. senator.

Numerous private schools were established during the territorial period, and after statehood 91,120 acres were set aside for a system of public schools. The General Assembly authorized two seminaries for teacher training in 1851, and two years later the East Florida Seminary, to which the University of Florida traces its origins, opened in Ocala. A West Florida Seminary, from which Florida State University claims descent, opened in Tallahassee in 1857.

The first newspaper of the territorial period was the *Florida Gazette*, published in St. Augustine in 1821. Papers of the time were small, consisting mostly of advertisements. In one year, Tallahassee had eleven such papers,

David Levy Yulee (1810–86) was one of Florida's foremost promoters and developers during the territorial and early statehood periods. He arrived in Florida from the West Indies with his father, Moses Elias Levy, in 1821. His father, the first prominent Jew in the peninsula, acquired large landholdings in what became Alachua County. David entered the politics of the new U.S. territory, became a delegate to the constitutional convention of 1838, territorial delegate to Congress in 1841, and, when statehood came, U.S. senator in 1845–51 and 1855–61. No one had worked harder to bring Florida into the Union, but he supported secession and served in the Confederate Congress, 1861–65. His economic development activities were best represented by the cross-state Florida Railroad that he completed in 1861 from Cedar Key on the Gulf to Fernandina on the Atlantic. The family name is perpetuated in Levy County and the town of Yulee.

Apalachicola ten, and Key West six. Many of the editors held public office or were independently influential in public affairs.

Churches of many denominations took root in the environment of religious liberty first declared here by the

A camera view looking north on Hospital (Avilés) Street in St. Augustine in the 1850s takes in the assembled winter guests of Miss Louisa Fatio's boardinghouse, at left. Northern visitors such as these were called "strangers" by local residents. Many came to the city for health reasons, particularly those who were "patients of a consumptive habit." The visitors profited, no doubt, from the relatively warm climate, the fresh sea breezes, the winter vegetables, and orange juice. Said one city booster, "Those who arrive there in an invalescent state, never fail to derive immediate benefit from its temperature and restorative air; and pulmonary patients experience a remarkable relief." Three hundred such "strangers" were in the city by the date of this photo. The original owner of the boardinghouse was Andrés Ximénez, hence its name today, the Ximénez-Fatio House.

British in their occupation and reaffirmed under American law: Anglicans, or Episcopalians, in St. Augustine and Methodists in Pensacola in 1821; Baptists in Nassau County in 1821 and in Bethlehem in 1825; and Presbyterians in St. Augustine in 1824. Jews had been in Pensacola since the 1760s and in St. Augustine since the 1780s. Roman Catholics, of course, had lived in the state since the earliest Spanish occupation, but in the mid-nineteenth century their numbers were small.

Writers of the period included Daniel G. Brinton and George Fairbanks, who both wrote histories of Florida; Buckingham Smith, who translated Florida-related documents in Spanish archives; Caroline Lee Hentz, novelist of plantation life; Dr. Wentworth Chapman, author of *Flora of the Southern United States*; and Dr. John Gorrie, a frequent contributor to medical journals. Gorrie, of Apalachicola, is best remembered for his invention in 1848 of an ice-making machine, an offshoot of his attempt to cool the hospital rooms of his feverish patients. Refrigeration and air-conditioning would be his legacy in the next century.

Statehood led to rapid economic growth in Florida during the antebellum years. The population grew from 70,000 persons in 1845 to 140,424 in 1860, of whom 40 percent were slaves, which suggests the principal supports of the economy: cotton and forest products. Planters concentrated in middle Florida dominated the life of the state. Cattle raising, Florida's oldest industry, continued in what are now Hillsborough, Manatee, Polk, Hernando, Orange, and—its place of origin—Alachua counties. Railroads became a major interest after 1845, at which date only one line, from Tallahassee to St. Marks, was in operation. Subsequently lines were built from Jacksonville to Alligator (later Lake City) in 1860 and from Cedar Keys to Fernandina in 1861, the latter to carry out cedar for shipment to pencil factories in the north and Europe.

Secession

Florida had lived under four flags—Spanish, French, British, and American—and in 1861 would raise a fifth one. With Abraham Lincoln's election to the presidency in November 1860, mass meetings took place in many Florida towns to protest the expected Republican assault on the institution of slavery. "We say Resist," declared the Fernandina *East Floridian*. Most Florida whites said the same, as demonstrated in January 1861 when both houses of the

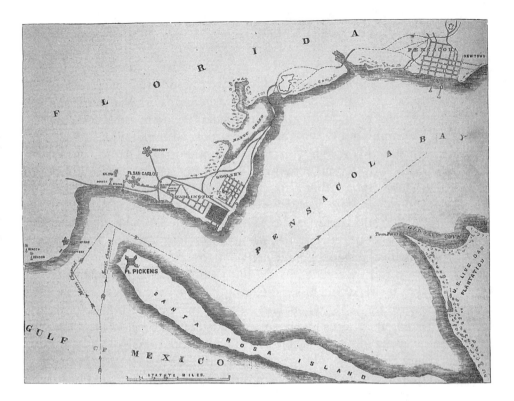

This depiction of Pensacola and its harbor at the outset of secession leading to the Civil War appeared in Harper's Weekly *in February 1861. Though secessionist troops occupied Forts McRee and Barrancas (San Carlos) as well as the Pensacola Navy Yard, Union forces managed to hold onto and reinforce the strategically placed Fort Pickens. Pickens twice exchanged artillery fire with the Confederate batteries and ground forces of the two sides clashed once, but the fort saw little significant action. The Confederates withdrew from their installations in May 1862. In the last years of the war Pickens's interior rooms served as a prison for military and political prisoners. In 1888 they would hold the captured Apache chief from Oklahoma, Geronimo, and his band.*

General Assembly unanimously passed a bill calling for a constitutional convention. That convention in turn, on January 10, 1861, adopted an Ordinance of Secession by which the independent "nation of Florida" withdrew from the American Union, the third state to do so, following South Carolina and Mississippi. The vote, sixty-two to seven, was observed throughout Florida by torchlight processions, bonfires, bell ringing, and general celebration. Less than a month later, when a confederacy was formed, Florida raised the stars and bars of the Confederate States of America.

Military action followed at once. During January, state troops seized federal property: the arsenal at Chattahoochee, Fort Clinch on Amelia Island, Fort Marion (San Marcos) at St. Augustine, and the navy yard at Pensacola. In the same month federal troops occupied Fort Taylor at Key West and Fort Jefferson on Garden Key in the Dry Tortugas; both forts would remain in Union possession throughout the war. At another important federal emplacement, at Pensacola Bay, U.S. forces withdrew from two mainland forts, McRee and Barrancas, to Fort Pickens on Santa Rosa Island, which guarded the bay's entrance. Fort Pickens was so weakly garrisoned and armed it might easily have been captured by a rebel attack, but Confederate leaders feared that the resulting bloodshed might cause immediate war. By April 12, 1861, when Fort Sumter in South Carolina was fired on, Pickens had been reinforced and a successful attack was no longer possible. Pickens would remain in Union hands throughout the war and would serve as federal headquarters in Florida. Most of the conflict during the first year of the war occurred at Pensacola. Several raids and two artillery bombardments were exchanged between Pickens and mainland Confederate forces. In May 1862, the Confederates withdrew and left the city, by then a ghost town, in federal hands.

During 1862 federal forces began consolidating their control of coastal Florida, seizing Fernandina, Jacksonville, St. Augustine, Tampa, Cedar Keys, and Apalachicola. Jacksonville would be invaded four different times and suffer burnings by both federals and Confederates. Control of the coastline enabled federal blockade ships to reduce importation of foodstuffs, supplies, and munitions desperately needed by the Confederacy. Blockade running continued throughout the war, as a variety of rebel vessels made the passage from Havana and the British Bahamas to deposit cargoes in Florida's countless bays, inlets, rivers, and inland waterways. On return trips the boats would take cotton, turpentine, and tobacco for trade.

Confederate strategy was to hold the interior of Florida, according to a plan devised by General Robert E. Lee on two wartime visits to Fernandina. It was critical to the Confederacy that Florida's food-producing farmlands and cattle ranches be protected. At one point cattle were being driven north from the ranches at the rate of 600 a week. Some cattlemen in South Florida played both sides, selling to the highest bidder whether it was the Confederacy, the Union garrisons at Fort Myers and Key West, or the Cubans at Havana. Equally precious to the Confederacy was salt, for without it meat could not be preserved. Salt was needed also in the preparation of hides for tanning in the manufacture of leather. The principal saltworks, where men boiled seawater in huge kettles and sheet-iron boilers, were located around St. Andrews Bay (near present-day Panama City) and Apalachee Bay in Taylor County. At its height the war-created industry employed 5,000 men, all exempt from military service. Union blockade squadrons sought out and destroyed the saltworks from time to time, but the installations were quickly rebuilt.

The main battles of the war in Florida took place in the interior and were occasioned by Union threats to the food-producing regions. In February 1864 a federal force of 5,500 men marched out of Jacksonville toward Lake City. Confederate General Joseph Finegan, with a reinforced army of 5,200 men, met the invaders at Olustee, thirteen miles from Lake City, and scored a decisive victory in a pitched battle lasting from noon until six o'clock on the evening of February 20. The federals lost 203 killed, 1,152 wounded, and 506 missing; Finegan counted 93 killed, 847 wounded, and 6 missing. It was the single major engagement of the war in Florida. The Union defeat and retreat at Olustee were followed soon by federal embarrassments at Gainesville, Cedar Keys, and Natural Bridge, which crossed the St. Marks River near Tallahassee. Often young boys and old men in home-guard units were responsible for the Confederate successes, although one such "cradle and grave" company could not prevent the Union's recapture of Marianna.

At war's end, Tallahassee was the only Confederate capital east of the Mississippi that had not been captured. Florida had given 15,000 men to Confederate service, about a third of whom lost their lives in combat or from disease. It is estimated that 1,200 white Floridians and, in the last years of the war, an equal number of freed slaves served in

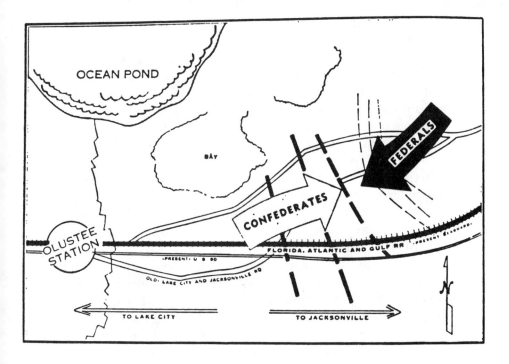

The Battle of Olustee on February 20, 1864, was the lone major battle fought on Florida soil during the Civil War. It was precipitated by a Union invasion of the interior out of Jacksonville in the direction of Lake City. The Federals' intentions were to acquire a source of cotton, lumber, timber, and turpentine, to cut off the Confederacy's supply of Florida beef and pork, and to find black recruits for the Union army. The 5,500-man Federal force was met a few miles east of Olustee by an equal number of Confederates, and the two sides clashed from noon until after six o'clock. The action resulted in a Confederate victory, as the Federals made a gradual withdrawal, leaving behind much of their weapons and ammunition. A rout was prevented by the gallant performance of two all-black regiments (represented in the engraving on page 44, right foreground), the Fifty-fourth Massachusetts (of Battery Wagner fame) and the First Carolina. The Federals lost 203 killed, 1,152 wounded, the Confederates, 93 killed, 847 wounded.

the Union army. Numerous Floridians achieved high command and distinction in the conflict, among them Stephen R. Mallory of Key West, successor to David Levy Yulee as U.S. senator before the war, who was secretary of the navy in the cabinet of President Jefferson Davis; General Edmund Kirby-Smith of St. Augustine, who ended the war as one of the seven full generals of the army and one of the last to surrender to Union forces; and William Wing Loring, also of St. Augustine, who was senior major general in active field service at the time of Appomattox. Florida's women endured the war heroically; they rolled bandages, made uniforms, nursed the wounded, and, in the absence of their men, managed the estates and farms. To the surprise of many, loyal black slaves remained to help the women—the slave insurrection that had been expected and feared never happened. On May 10, 1865, Union troops occupied Tallahassee without opposition. Florida's governor throughout most of the conflict, John Milton of Jackson County, was not present to see the invaders march through his capital. Believing that "death would be preferable to reunion," he committed suicide the month before.

Reconstruction

A way of life had ended. For African-Americans, nearly half the state's population, freedom had come at last, but for those who left their masters and mistresses for the towns and federal army camps there were at first no jobs, only promises. Without money or homes, many died from malnutrition, exposure, and lack of medical attention. For white Floridians one representative of the old order described things aptly when he said, "The world is upside down." Farmers struggled to make their untended fields productive, merchants scrambled for goods and for capital, and the state government stood still in humiliating confusion. Within a short time, however, both blacks and whites would right themselves, and Florida, least damaged physi-

White and black immigrants to Florida after the Civil War found a still largely undeveloped frontier. Mostly small-time farmers from Georgia, Alabama, and the Carolinas, the whites came with livestock, farming implements, and household goods. Their pride, pluck, and gritty self-reliance created the culture that came to be called "Cracker." The increase in black residents raised their proportion of the population to 47 percent. In their new status as freedmen, most sought employment as laborers on the plantations. The highest concentration of people continued to be found in the "middle Florida" cotton counties, where population density was eighteen to forty-five inhabitants per square mile. The whole of South Florida (from today's Interstate 4 on down) had fewer than two inhabitants per square mile. One traveled the northern half of the state by slow oxcart or bouncing stagecoach over sandy rut roads, by the few existing railroad lines, or by steamboat. In the south there were footpaths only, no rails.

cally of the southern states, would rebound dramatically to economic and political health. Unfortunately for the blacks, their share in the resurgence would not last long.

The first meaningful assistance given the free blacks was administered through the Freedmen's Bureau, established by Congress in March 1865 to supply rations, to organize black schools and orphanages, to advise adult freedmen of their rights and duties, to regularize marriages, and to encourage the former slaves to return to work. By January 1866 most blacks were returning to the farms and plantations to begin crop planting. Christian denominations in the North sent both clerical and lay missionaries to teach in black schools and to instruct the black populations, in many places for the first time, in the Christian faith professed by their former masters.

Florida's first postwar state government was not nearly so enlightened and generous toward the blacks as were the Freedmen's Bureau and the northern churches. After the inauguration of Governor David S. Walker in January 1866, the legislature passed harsh and discriminatory laws directed against blacks. Emphasizing such crimes as rape, insurrection, and vagrancy, these so-called Black Codes represented an attempt by the former slaveholders to reinstitute the slave system in fact if not in law. Similar initiatives were taken in other southern states, and their effect was the opposite of what was intended. Congress in quick reaction extended the life of the Freedmen's Bureau, then passed the Civil Rights Act of 1866 and the very similar Fourteenth Amendment. Because Congress had as yet no southern members, it replaced the almost pro-South form of Reconstruction proposed by Lincoln and conducted by his successor, President Andrew Johnson, with a congressional Reconstruction designed by radical Republicans to discipline recalcitrant southern state governments.

Radical Republican representatives, in and out of the Freedmen's Bureau, came to Florida to form secret black societies and to organize black voters, who had suffrage by congressional mandate. Their success was manifest in the results of the 1868 elections, when sixteen Republicans but only eight Democrats (the party of the white southern conservatives) were elected to the state senate and thirty-seven Republicans but only fifteen Democrats to the lower house. Of the fifty-three Republicans, thirteen were "carpetbaggers," northerners who had come south to take advantage of Florida's new opportunities, twenty-one were "scalawags," southerners who had supported the Union, and nineteen were blacks. Among the black legislators was a preacher, Jonathan C. Gibbs, who would become secretary of state in the cabinet of Governor Harrison Reed. Other black leaders of this period and later were Josiah T. Walls, John Wallace, and Henry S. Harmon.

Governor Reed, a native of New Hampshire, was a newcomer to the state. His Republican administration, the first

This steel engraving of St. Francis Street in St. Augustine was executed by the English artist Harry Fenn, a well-known illustrator and founder of the American Water-Color Society. First published in 1872, the engraving shows, to the right, the González-Alvarez House. Research has disclosed continuous occupancy of the site since the early 1600s. The coquina walls of this structure were raised soon after the town was burned during the British siege of 1702. Tomás Gonzáles y Hernández with his wife, Francisca de Guevara, lived in the house from 1727 to 1763. A National Historic Landmark, the house was restored and is maintained by the St. Augustine Historical Society.

civil authority to replace postwar military rule and martial law, lasted for five stormy years, during which Reed succeeded in angering both the conservative white Florida natives and the radical Republicans of his own party. In the process he survived four separate attempts at impeachment. His successor in 1873, Ossian B. Hart, was the first native Floridian to be elected to the governorship. He died within a year and was succeeded by Lieutenant Governor Marcellus L. Stearns, a Maine Republican.

The 1876 elections were particularly hard fought. Stearns was nominated by the Republicans; the Democrats, by now resurgent, put forward George F. Drew, a native of New Hampshire who had lived in both Georgia and Florida. Black voters were grossly exploited by both sides, and the actual balloting was marked by widespread chicanery and fraud, again by both sides. Although Stearns emerged the apparent winner—and Florida's four electoral votes went to Rutherford B. Hayes, giving him the presidency by one electoral vote over Samuel J. Tilden—the Florida Supreme Court, acting on appeal from Drew, ordered a recount, with the result that Drew was given the governorship by a margin of 195 votes.

With Drew's inauguration in 1877, two-party politics came to an end in Florida. So did the presence of federal troops. Southern white conservatism was now in a position to restore the political and social values that reconstructionists had challenged. Democrats by party, the leaders of the restoration came to be called Bourbons, a derogatory term meant to associate them with the Bourbon kings of France who had learned nothing from the past. Where northern radicals had attempted to build a political base on the votes of blacks and lower-class whites, the new leaders, eager to keep the freedmen "in their place," created an all-white unity that would place Florida squarely in the Democratic South then forming. Though their condition between the years 1868 and 1877 was arguably better than it would be for the next three-quarters of a century, blacks had received back from the Republican party less than they had given it. And now, under the Democrats, they would begin to lose the effective exercise of such rights as they had left, including that of suffrage. The theory of white supremacy would permeate statutory, even constitutional, law. Hooded riders, such as the Ku Klux Klan members, would spread intimidation and violence in black districts. By 1887 a series of Jim Crow laws enacted by the legislature would ensure that the state's blacks would be subjugated to a status suggestive of social if not complete legal and physical bondage. And by 1890, because of poll taxes and multiple ballot boxes, most blacks would no longer vote. The failure of this part of Reconstruction would not be repaired until the second half of the twentieth century.

For the whites, Reconstruction would be recalled for several generations as a source of shame and bitterness. Most

Paddlewheel steamboats plied the scenic rivers of Florida's interior, such as the St. Johns, the Suwannee, and the Apalachicola. Here, the Metamora *reveals to visitors the deep green beauty of the wilderness along the Ocklawaha River. President (and former general) Ulysses S. Grant made such an excursion up the Ocklawaha, in 1880, aboard the steamboat* Osceola. *A writer who accompanied Grant's party recorded, "The steamers that thread the very narrow and wonderfully crooked waters of that stream are each an aquatic curiosity. Built especially for the route, they are altogether unique. Upon the roof of the wheel-house of our special steamer was a large iron box where a bonfire of pitch-pine knots lighted up the scenery by night."*

scorned "Negro rule" and resented it as the apparent northern desire for revenge, while others lamented the political wrangling, the exploitation, and the corruption that plainly abounded. It can be argued, however, that the period overall was one of political advancement. Though the product of partisan divisions, the state constitution of 1868 was an enlightened document, the best that Florida would have in the century. In other respects, too—the criminal code, state services, and public schools—Reconstruction leaders achieved notable gains. Apart from the decisive social issue of racial equality, they shared the goals of the native Democrats: economic growth and development. Once the backwater of the rural South, postwar Florida promised to become a boom state, and every white

Cheyenne Indians confined at Fort Francis Marion (as the United States had renamed Castillo de San Marcos) at St. Augustine in 1875. Members of a group of Plains Indians from the American West that included not only Cheyenne but also Arapaho, Kiowa, and Comanche Indians who refused to accept confinement in reservations, they had been captured by the U.S. Army and sent in chains by railway to St. Augustine for imprisonment. Southern musician and poet Sidney Lanier watched the arrival of the seventy-one captives: "As they stepped out of the cars [of the train], and folded their ample blankets about them, there was a large dignity and majestic sweep about their movements that made me much desire to salute their grave excellencies." Their imprisonment ended in 1878, but another, larger group of Chiricahua Apaches took their place in 1886.

man with or without means, Republican or Democrat, wanted a part of it. Between 1860 and 1880 the population swelled to 269,493, an increase of 90 percent. Not since the first Spanish period had so many residents been born in the state: 64.4 percent (a figure never equaled afterward).

The Bourbon Era

Governor Drew's inaugural address summarized what would be called Florida's Bourbon era: "That government will be most highly esteemed that gives the greatest protection to individual and industrial enterprises at the least expense to the taxpayer." For the next decades Florida would attract investors and immigrants, allow for unrestricted development and management of the state's resources by private individuals and corporations, keep taxes to a minimum, and limit expenditures to education and social services. Reform would give way to coastal and interior land development. For that to happen, however, Florida's new laissez-faire government would have to offer considerable land grants for railroad construction. Yet bondholders, supported by court order, held a mortgage on those public lands that would be suitable and necessary for the railroads.

The problem was solved by Drew's successor in office, William D. Bloxham, who in 1881 arranged for the sale of 4 million acres of uplands and swamplands to Philadelphia capitalist Hamilton Disston at twenty-five cents an acre. While Disston engaged in the work of draining and selling his land, Bloxham paid off the state's creditors and opened up millions of acres for railroad construction.

When Bloxham assumed office in 1881, there were 550 miles of railroad in operation. By 1891 there were 2,566 miles and by 1900 there were 3,500 miles. This remarkable growth was supported by the governors of the period, Bloxham (1881–85), Edward A. Perry (1885–89), Francis P. Fleming (1889–93), Henry L. Mitchell (1893–97), and Bloxham again (1897–1901). The accomplishment itself was the work principally of three industrialists: William D. Chipley, Henry B. Plant, and Henry M. Flagler. Chipley, a

A stylized photograph showing orange picking and packing (but not, it appears, much joy) at Maitland in the 1880s. The orange was introduced to this country by the Spaniards at St. Augustine, where, by the time Florida became a U.S. territory, the city was producing an annual crop of nearly two million oranges. After a prolonged freeze destroyed the groves there in 1835, orange production shifted to the interior, westward and south. Even those groves in Central Florida counties below the "frost line," as the one shown here, did not escape a catastrophic freeze in 1895, and, with the region's economy in collapse, many settlers left the area, some leaving behind fully furnished houses. Those who could afford to wait several years replanted their groves. Those who could not started the decorative fern industry that today exports potted and fresh-cut foliage to all of North America and Europe.

Rail passengers enjoy an excursion on the Jacksonville, St. Augustine & Halifax River Railway Co. tracks in the 1880s. The narrow gauge steam locomotive line, eighty miles in length, took passengers and freight from the south bank of the St. Johns River at Jacksonville to a point at or near St. Augustine and finally to a turnaround fifteen miles in from the coast near the headwaters of the Halifax River. From twenty-four short rail lines such as this one Henry M. Flagler incorporated the Florida East Coast Railway Company, Flagler System, beginning in 1895. By 1916 the FEC had 522 miles of mainline from Jacksonville to Key West and 217 miles of branch lines.

native of Georgia, was general manager of the Louisville and Nashville Company. By 1882 he constructed 161 miles of rail called the Jacksonville, Pensacola, and Mobile Railroad. He invested heavily in Pensacola and became for a time the city's mayor. As Chipley connected the Panhandle with the rest of developed Florida, so Henry B. Plant, a Connecticut Yankee, joined the Atlantic port of Jacksonville with the Gulf port of Tampa. At Tampa, to encourage passenger travel, Plant built the exotic Tampa Bay Hotel (now the University of Tampa). Because his line traversed central Florida, Plant made possible the first development of the

Members of the 1887 state House of Representatives assemble on the capitol steps in Tallahassee. Six African-American members were among the last to serve in this body, which in the same year enacted Jim Crow legislation mandating separation of the races. A constitution adopted two years earlier authorized a poll tax, and by 1890 most blacks were excluded from the voting booth as well as from the legislature. Reconstruction was over, and so were the chances of freedmen to establish a secure place in Florida government and society. No black would serve again in the legislature until Joe Lang Kershaw, a civics teacher from Coral Gables, was elected to the house in 1968. The first black woman member was Gwen Sawyer Cherry, representative from Dade County, elected in 1970.

citrus industry in that part of the state. Three years after Plant's death in 1899, his Florida line would merge with the Atlantic Coast Line. John S. Williams, a Virginian, purchased and built six hundred miles of rail in Florida, which in 1903 would merge with Seaboard Air Line Railroad.

By far the most celebrated railroad magnate of the period was Henry Morrison Flagler. A partner of John D. Rockefeller, he had made a great fortune before moving to Florida

In 1887–88 Henry M. Flagler's Ponce de Leon Hotel rose on the western edge of St. Augustine. The developer's young Beaux-Arts architects John M. Carrère and Thomas W. Hastings created a lavish Spanish-Moorish fantasy that quickly became the most exclusive winter resort in the nation. No less ornate were the hotel's interiors, designed by Bernard Maybeck, which featured finely crafted frescoes, mosaics, carved wood, Tiffany windows, and Tojetti ceilings. Flagler later opened two other hotels nearby, the Alcazar and the Córdova. Carrère and Hastings went on to distinguished national careers. Marble busts of the two men are displayed in the foyer of their acclaimed New York Public Library on Fifth Avenue in Manhattan.

in the 1880s. In St. Augustine he built a magnificent tourist hotel, the Ponce de Leon (now Flagler College), to accommodate northerners who wished to take advantage of Florida's winters. Completed in 1888, the hotel, the first major structure in the country to be built of poured concrete, would become in its first quarter century a mecca for affluent and important travelers, including four U.S. presidents. Flagler built a railroad, the Florida East Coast, to

The good old summertime at Cedar Keys on the upper Gulf Coast in 1896. The area prospered in the post–Civil War years from cedar logging and fishing. Population peaked at 2,000 in 1885 when three pencil factories cut red cedar into pencil stock and shipped the product across the Florida Railroad to the port at Fernandina for transport to the North and Europe, where it was processed into pencils. The three factories consumed 300 logs a day, which, when cut, became 1,157,000 miles of lead pencils annually. By the 1890s the cedar forests were exhausted. So were the green turtles, oysters, and other sea delicacies that the Keys had shipped to big city restaurants. In the same year that this photograph was taken, a fierce hurricane, accompanied by a tidal wave, destroyed the factories and much of the town. By the end of the century the population would be 700.

bring his clientele south from Jacksonville. In 1894 he extended the line to West Palm Beach, and, at neighboring Palm Beach, he erected two other resort hotels, the Royal Poinciana and the Breakers (twice burned and rebuilt), as well as a $2.5 million marble mansion for himself and his third wife to which he gave the name "Whitehall."

The winter of 1894–95 brought severely damaging freezes to most of Florida, except for the pioneer village of Miami. Flagler had already developed plans to push his railroad south to that city, but he was waiting for two principal landowners, Julia D. Tuttle and William B. Brickell, to deed him half of their property, hers north of the Miami River, his

Mrs. Susie Bruton, teacher, and her pupils at the one-room schoolhouse in Alva, on the north bank of the Caloosahatchee River, near Fort Myers, in 1897. The teacher's attire was a white shirtwaist buttoned up the front, a black, dark blue, or gray serge skirt, and buttoned high-top shoes. The boys wore cotton shirts and homespun trousers, the girls wore red and blue gingham that was checked or striped with white. The children's diet included grass-fed beef from the nearby ranges, pork, ham, sausage, and bacon; vegetables such as okra, string beans, white squash, turnips, mustard greens, and tomatoes; hoecake (corn bread) and biscuits with cane syrup; whole milk or buttermilk; and—if they were good—blackberry cobbler or sweet potato pie.

south. The deeds were made and, according to a story (probably true), Mrs. Tuttle sent Flagler an orange blossom cutting in dampened cotton to convince the railroad magnate that the freeze had not touched Miami. Three hundred settlers watched the first train chug into town in April 1896. Though Flagler expressed his belief that Miami itself would never be more than a "fishing village," he did build a resort hotel there, the Royal Palm. After the turn of the century, in an act that required engineering genius, enormous capital, and personal courage, he would extend his rails across 128 miles of water and keys to Key West.

The typical Florida cowman, like Tom Johnson, shown here in the 1890s, was often called a "cow hunter," since much of his time was spent searching for cattle in heavily wooded ranges or palmetto prairies. His "cracker" or "marsh" pony descended from a breed introduced by rancheros in Spanish times. Both horse and rider were accustomed to eighteen hours of steady riding, broken only by stops at the long covered oxcart that hauled the cowman's grub: biscuit, bacon and lard, salt pork, syrup, and coffee—three or four quarts a day per man. When a drive ended at, say, Punta Rassa (near Fort Myers), the cowmen would take their pay in gold, drink Cuban rum at fifty cents a gallon, and let off steam by firing their revolvers through the floors of their barracks.

The railroads dramatically changed Florida's communications, especially along the eastern seaboard. Notably affected were the mails. Prior to the completion of Flagler's line to Miami, mail between that city and Palm Beach and several points in between was carried by barefoot mailmen who walked the beach three days each way. The railroads opened up Florida to numerous commercial and agricultural opportunities. Along with the pleasure-seekers who crowded the coastal hotels, farmers, laborers, merchants, and professional people poured into Florida's cities and rural areas. Settlement and drainage turned the southern quarter of the peninsula into a thriving agricultural region.

New York volunteer troops at Port Tampa in June 1898 wait to board ships (in background) that will take them to Cuba during the Spanish-American War. Lacking khaki cloth, the army sent men like these to steaming Tampa, and then to hotter Cuba, in the heavy blue uniforms of winter garrison duty. A correspondent for the Washington Post *in Tampa reported that "a lemonade man, equipped with a bucket and two tin cups, can make $25 a day." At Tampa and the other Florida campsites diseases such as typhoid fever took the lives of many volunteers, most of them before they boarded ship or after they returned from battle. Actual combat losses in Cuba numbered 379, but disease took 4,784. Clara Barton, founder of the American Red Cross, tended to the sick in Tampa.*

The "orange mania" swept the northern central counties until the freeze of 1895 caused the citrus industry to focus on land south of the frost line. With the railroads logging was no longer dependent on navigable rivers to move logs to mills. Cigar factories grew rapidly in number at Key West and particularly at Tampa.

Cattle ranching expanded, especially in the southwest where for a time the Peace River Valley rivaled the Wild West for scenes of stampedes, rustling, and gunplay. The Florida cowmen worked their herds with eighteen-foot-long braided buckskin whips that, when cracked, sounded like rifle shots across the palmetto prairies. According to one theory, it was this whip-cracking that gave rise to "Crackers" as a sobriquet for native Floridians.

In 1898 Tampa's population exploded briefly as 23,000 U.S. troops, including Colonel Theodore Roosevelt and his Rough Riders, made the port city their embarkation point

These Seminole Indians, photographed for the first time at Pine Island west of Fort Lauderdale about 1900, were native to Florida. Their ancestors had come into the peninsula from Georgia and Alabama in the eighteenth century following the destruction by British-led forces of Florida's original, or Spanish Mission, Indians. Three separate groups constituted the Seminoles. Two, of Lower Creek origin, spoke Miccosukee. The third, Upper Creeks, also called Cow Creeks, spoke Muskogee. As different as Spanish and Portuguese, the two languages required interpreters for understanding. The colorful patchwork Seminole dress was unique among American Indians, as were their "chickee" huts of cypress pole and palmetto thatch, shown here at rear.

or invasion of Cuba during the Spanish-American War. Other Florida cities, too, were campsites or reinforced bases, including Lakeland, Fernandina, Jacksonville, Miami, Key West, and Pensacola. After the short war Florida's bullish economy returned to normal, but word spread by returning soldiers about the state's attractions spurred further immigration.

With the exception of the great freeze, a hurricane in 1896 that destroyed Cedar Keys, and two yellow fever epidemics (Key West, Manatee, Tampa, and Plant City in 1887 and Jacksonville in 1888), the Bourbon era counted nothing but successes and good times. As the change of centuries drew near, Floridians took understandable pride in the growth and development that had taken place. It was clear that Florida's

Shortly after noon on May 3, 1901, fiber laid out to dry outside a factory at Beaver and Davis streets in Jacksonville caught fire. A fresh west-northwest wind blew the sparks onto neighboring buildings where wooden roofs were as combustible as tinder because of a long drought. The flames spread from building to building as rapidly, it was said, as a man could walk. By 7:30 P.M., when the wind died, all but a small section of Jacksonville's downtown was destroyed and ten thousand people were left homeless. It was the most devastating fire ever to hit a southern city. This view after the fire was from the top of Federal Building looking east down Forsyth Street. By 1919 a sparkling new downtown with "skyscrapers" had risen over the ashes.

economic position was different from that of her sister states from the old Confederacy. Though once an emerging cotton state, after the war Florida had moved away from cotton, and her population, predominantly southern in origin, became engaged in different activities: timber, cattle, citrus, winter vegetables—and tourism. Before the war Florida had been advertised to northerners for health reasons, and as one hotel resident at St. Augustine in the 1850s observed, "You hear the funereal cough all over the house, and in the parlor they loll at full length on the sofas and expectorate almost constantly." In the last decades of the century Florida attracted more healthy people than invalids as thousands of northerners came into the state simply for travel, rest, and recreation. Originally called "strangers," the travelers now were called "visitors"; in the twentieth century they would

This photograph, taken in 1904, of Seabreeze Beach at Daytona, represents a typical nineteenth-century display of horse-drawn carriages. There is not an automobile in sight, though by this date no fewer than sixty of the new-fangled vehicles could be counted in the city, and the wide Daytona beaches were the scene of celebrated automobile speed trials. Here, in 1903, Alexander Winton drove his gasoline-powered "Bullet" at sixty-eight miles per hour. Much faster vehicles were to come. The state legislature passed laws limiting the vehicles to "reasonable speed" on roads, without specifying what was reasonable. Other new laws required drivers to give "ample signal or warning" lest they frighten pedestrians or horses.

be called "tourists." By both train and ship they arrived to winter in the new seacoast hotels or to explore Florida's rivers, such as the St. Johns, Suwannee, and Ocklawaha, in steamboats outfitted with staterooms and salons. Many stayed or returned to build homes.

Tampa was joined on the Gulf Coast by the new towns of Clearwater, St. Petersburg, Tarpon Springs, Sarasota, and Fort Myers. Joining Palm Beach and Miami on the south Atlantic were Fort Pierce and Fort Lauderdale. Inland, Or-

The graduating class of 1904 at Florida State Normal Industrial School in Tallahassee, which became after 1909 Florida Agricultural and Mechanical College and after 1953 Florida A & M University. These graduates were Robert William Butler, John Adams Cromartie, Arthur Rudolf Grant, Rufus Jason Hawkins, Rosa Belle Lee, Sara Grace Moore, Winifred Leone Perry, Walter Carolus Smith, Margaret Guinervere Wilkins, Margaret Adelle Yellowhair, and Walter Theodore Young. In the same year, 1904, Mary McLeod Bethune opened the Daytona Normal and Industrial Institute for Girls, which in 1923 merged with the Cookman Institute, of Jacksonville, to form what became Bethune-Cookman College, at Daytona Beach, in 1923.

lando was the largest city in central Florida, and the new towns of DeLand, Sanford, Kissimmee, Lakeland, and Bartow were growing fast. Far to the south, Key West was a bustling international port of call for ships engaged in Atlantic, Caribbean, and Gulf trade. The most cosmopolitan of Florida's cities and for a time its largest, it had little contact with the rest of the peninsula, not to mention the Panhandle. By 1900 the state's population numbered 528,000, an increase of 42 percent in a decade. Jacksonville was contesting with Key West and Pensacola to become the

No governor brought a more variegated background to the office than did Napoleon Bonaparte Broward (1905–9), shown here with his family on the mansion steps in Tallahassee. He had been a logger, a farmhand, a steamboat crew member, a Newfoundland cod fisherman, a lumberman, a phosphate mine developer, sheriff of Duval County, and a boat pilot. In the last capacity, he ran a mail and passenger steamboat service and, in a celebrated seagoing tugboat, The Three Friends, made eight filibustering trips through a Spanish blockade to deliver contraband guns to Cuban revolutionaries in the 1890s. Broward and his wife, Annie Isabel Douglass, had eight daughters and one son. Elizabeth, shown here on the lap of her mother, was the first child born to an incumbent governor of the state.

largest city; ten years later it would have nearly double the population of each of the other two cities. Because of the rapid development of eastern and southern Florida, a movement mounted to move the capital from Tallahassee to a more central location. In a statewide referendum held in 1900, however, 52 percent of those voting favored keeping the capital where it was. And there—despite several later and similar attempts to move it—it has stayed since.

Magnus Delacy Peavy and farmhands in front of his tobacco barn at Havana (northwest of Talla-hassee) about 1910. The town, where cultivation of Cuban tobacco began in 1829, was named for the Cuban capital. Here in the antebellum cotton country a typical farm in 1910 might have milk cows and barnyard poultry, hogs, sweet potatoes, watermelons, some pecan trees, tobacco, perhaps corn and peanuts, and some rows of short staple cotton. With a diversified operation the North Florida farmer was protected against crop failure. Much of the former cotton land around nearby Tallahassee re-turned to forest, and in the following decades northern industrialists purchased large acreages for hunting preserves—"quail plantations."

Modern Florida Begins

Not only the new century but also modern Florida began with the emergence of Napoleon Bonaparte Broward. Three times sheriff of his native Duval County, he was elected to the legislature in 1900 where he espoused the cause of the common man, especially in the rural districts. His strong Jeffersonian emphasis on farm-labor values had been anticipated by a Populist movement in Florida that

Henry M. Flagler (circled) is shown at the arrival in Key West on January 22, 1912, of the first Florida East Coast passenger train to pass across the overseas rail line that he had built from the mainland. The Key West Extension united the long-isolated island city with the rest of Florida and was hailed by speakers at the 1912 completion celebrations as the "Eighth Wonder of the World." Flagler rightly regarded it as the crowning achievement of his life. The prosperity expected from the extension by Key West never materialized, however, during the two decades that followed. Badly damaged in the Labor Day hurricane of 1935, the rail line was replaced by an automobile "overseas highway" that traverses forty-two bridges, one of them seven miles long.

Pilot Anthony "Tony" Jannus waves as he lands his Benoist Airboat at Tampa in 1914 to complete the inaugural flight of the world's first regularly scheduled passenger airline service, which linked Tampa and St. Petersburg. The service lasted three months. Lincoln Beachey is credited with having made the state's first flight in a heavier-than-air craft, a Curtiss biplane, at Orlando, in 1910. Aviation schools opened soon afterward at Pensacola, Jacksonville, St. Augustine, and Miami. In September 1922 Aviation Lieutenant James H. "Jimmy" Doolittle (of later Tokyo Raid fame) lifted off from Pablo Beach, now Jacksonville Beach, in a DeHavilland DH-4 biplane and landed twenty-two hours and thirty minutes later in San Diego, California—the first pilot to cross the continent in less than a day.

dated from before 1890, when national farm and labor alliances held a national convention in Ocala and adopted a platform called the "Ocala Demands." Though Populists never achieved a political majority in Florida, their ideals persisted into the new century. In 1904, against formidable opposition from conservative Bourbon politicians, major corporations, and urban newspapers, Broward was elected governor. The Progressive period in American politics had come to Florida.

In the one term that he served, Governor Broward called for compulsory education, state assistance to public schools, improvement of teachers' standards and salaries, regulation of child labor, food and drug inspection, fish and game conservation laws, forest protection, Everglades drainage, prison reform, and equitable apportionment of the legislature. His philosophy and programs, which had the effect of giving government back to the people, would be carried forward by his immediate successors, Albert W. Gilchrist (1909–13) and Park Trammell (1913–17). If Broward as governor is best remembered for any single act, it is for his leadership in initiating state-funded drainage of the Everglades to permit settlement of the southern part of the state. By 1921 sixteen settlements with two hundred people could be found in the Lake Okeechobee region.

Broward's administration began a decade when social changes in everyday life occurred more rapidly than in any earlier comparable period. Telephone service reached rural Florida and significantly altered the ways in which farming communities related to each other. For the first time it could be claimed that the average town of five hundred or more people had electric lights. Women cooked on stoves instead of in fireplaces. Businessmen used a contraption called a typewriter. Families ate Grape-nuts, grits instead of hominy, and baked goods made of self-rising flour. Postum and coffee, already ground, were sold in pound packages. Men got out of the frock coat and set aside their celluloid collars in favor of a softer cotton. Shunning country barbers who gave their services for free, men began to have their hair cut in "barber shops." Women changed their hair style from bangs to a slight curl and put away their homespun bonnets. Some wore skirts above the ankles and high-buttoned shoes. Backwoods houses began to sport brick chimneys instead of the stick-and-dirt structures that were common at the turn of the century, and store-bought manufactured furniture replaced homemade chairs, tables, and bedsteads.

By 1906 there were 296 automobiles in the state: Daytona had 74, Miami 38, Jacksonville 17, and Tampa 15. By 1913 there were no fewer than 15,000. Two years later, in Governor Trammell's administration, a State Road Department was created and hard-surface paving began on the secondary road system that we have today. The appearance of the automobile presaged the time, half a century later, when tourism, most of it by automobile, would be the state's leading industry. Aviation, the other great future means of visitor traffic, also took early root in Florida. During the three months of January–March 1914, the St. Petersburg–Tampa Airboat Line, with a Benoist aircraft piloted by Anthony Jannus, operated the world's first regularly scheduled (though short-lived) passenger and commercial freight air service.

Another sign of Florida's coming of age during the Broward era was the Buckman Act of 1905, which consolidated seven state-supported colleges and schools into four specialized institutions: the University of Florida at Gainesville (all male until 1947); the Florida State College for Women at Tallahassee (after 1947 the coeducational Florida State University); the State Normal School for Negroes at Tallahassee (after 1909 Florida Agricultural and Mechanical College and after 1953 Florida A & M University); and a School for the Deaf, Dumb, and Blind at St. Augustine. Private institutions of higher learning existed, in one form or another, by the first quarter of the century: Stetson University, which opened Florida's first law school in 1900; Florida Southern College (its name after 1935); Rollins College; Bethune-Cookman College; Edward Waters College; the Florida Normal and Industrial Institute; and the University of Miami, which would open in 1925. For most of Florida's history as a state, the people chosen for high office were either men who had immigrated to the state with distinguished educational and professional backgrounds or native sons who had studied outside the state. Not until 1929 and the election of Stetson graduate Doyle E. Carlton would Florida have a native son from a native institution as governor.

At his inaugural in January 1917, Governor Sidney J. Catts rode in the car he had used in the campaign. Its banner read, "This is the Ford that got me there." To the editor of the Jacksonville Metropolis *Catts explained that, just as Broward had been elected governor on the issue of Everglades drainage, "I had to have a battle cry which would stir up the people, and after careful thought I decided to choose the Catholic question." When a priest, Father Patrick J. Bresnahan, asked him after the election why he had told so many lies about Catholics, Catts replied, "Brother, it was just politics." Catts's executive secretary in the governor's office was a Catholic (though she kept it quiet), and one of Catts's sons, with his father's approval, married a Catholic.*

Florida's dread turpentine camps, which existed from the end of Reconstruction to 1949, produced as much as 20 percent of the world's supply. Under peonage, or forced labor, nonconvict black workers were compelled to labor in the pine woods until certain "debts" were satisfied, which they never or rarely were. White woodsriders enforced the pernicious practice. The laborers' lot was substantially no different from that of their forefathers under slavery. In the 1940s a lawsuit charged that a similar debt peonage system, affecting migrant black canecutters, existed in the sugar fields around Lake Okeechobee in South Florida.

The election of Sidney J. Catts to the governorship in 1916 was interesting more for the fact that he *was* elected than for anything that he did during his term. With a platform not markedly different from those of the other candidates, he did not seem to espouse a particular political philosophy. Catts succeeded because he discovered and skillfully exploited latent religious and class prejudices in the rural population, particularly anti-Catholicism, this despite the fact that Roman Catholics accounted for only 3 percent of the state's population of 921,618. The first candidate in Florida to use an automobile in a political campaign, Catts crisscrossed the rural interior in a Model T Ford, making his colorful, earthy charges through a car-mounted loudspeaker—another innovation—to crowds that were at first curious, then enthusiastic, and often frenzied. His powers on the stump are still legendary. "The Florida Crackers have only three friends," he would roar, "God Almighty, Sears Roebuck, and Sidney J. Catts!" On some occasions he swung loaded pistols in both hands. By contrast, Catts as governor (1917–21) was serious, sedate, and conciliatory toward both Catholics and the Democratic leadership, whom he had opposed.

World War I and Prohibition

The United States declared war against Germany on April 6, 1917, four months after the start of the Catts administration. By the armistice of the following year, 42,030 Floridians were in the armed services, including two future governors, David Sholtz of Daytona Beach and Spessard Holland of Bartow. Another future governor, Millard F. Caldwell, entered the army from his native state of Tennessee. Over a thousand Florida men were killed in action, and eighteen received the Distinguished Service Cross. Shipyards at Jacksonville and Tampa increased the nation's seagoing tonnage, the state's forests yielded much-needed lumber and naval stores, and its farmlands contributed to the wartime breadbasket. At home, food and other commodities were scarce and expensive. When an influenza epidemic swept the state in 1918, nearly 30,000 people contracted the disease and 464 died; it returned to take 64 lives in 1919 and 79 in 1920.

Sheriff's deputies in Dade County display a night's haul of illegal liquor during Prohibition. Miami was a conduit for the banned liquids, which arrived on speedboats with slick hull designs and Liberty aircraft engines from Bimini or West End in the Bahamas and from distilleries in Cuba. Gun battles frequently occurred when government patrols intercepted the fast boats. One daring runner, D. W. "Red" Shannon, drove his Goose with a pungent cargo through the middle of a regatta in Biscayne Bay while being pursued by Coast Guardsmen firing a machine gun. No less swashbuckling were seaplane pilots who airlifted spirits to pick-up points in the Everglades.

Prohibition of the manufacture, sale, and use of alcoholic beverages came to Florida in advance of the Eighteenth Amendment and the Volstead Act of 1919. Most counties of the state were dry by local option when Catts came into office, and the new governor—who imbibed privately on occasion—made statewide adoption of prohibition a priority. Not surprisingly, the legislature ratified the Eighteenth Amendment. As the nation's "Noble Experiment" progressed, however, Florida, despite its mainly dry tradition, became a major conduit for illegal liquor importation

Down the new Dixie Highway from Chicago to Florida came the first "tin can tourists" in camper and tent-equipped Model T automobiles. Parking in open camps, as here in De Soto Park, Tampa, in December 1920, the northern "snowbirds" luxuriated under the Florida sun and shared their tinned meats and vegetables. Local merchants complained that they bought neither potatoes nor shoes, but the frugal campers were the advance guard of the mid-twenties Florida boom.

and, by some accounts, one of the wettest states in the nation. Whatever reservations native Floridians had about alcohol yielded frequently to a new, sophisticated climate of opinion introduced by tourists and lot buyers. The greatest enforcement problems developed in Hillsborough, Dade, Palm Beach, Duval, and Nassau counties. Nowhere did the experiment fail so spectacularly as in the city of Miami. There, close to Cuban distilleries and to the liquor-rich British Bahamas, smugglers, or rumrunners, operated fleets of ships and airplanes that deposited assorted brands of liquor and wine at selected coves and inlets on South Florida's shoreline. In Miami one saloon conducted its business within a stone's throw of police headquarters. It sported polished counters, brass handrails, and stocks of bottles set on wood shelves. A policeman stood on duty directly opposite its busy entrance.

Boom in Paradise

In the twenties, Florida would see its most remarkable growth explosion yet, most of it in the form of runaway land sales on the lower east coast, particularly in the new cities of subtropical Dade County. Blessed with a balmy climate that attracted denizens of frost and snow, increasingly accessible by car and train, and situated in a state that after 1924 imposed no income or inheritance tax, Miami and Miami Beach nearly burst from the influx of 1925, when 2.5 million people poured into Florida. The torrent exceeded anything the nation had seen in oil booms or free-land stampedes. Given good weather, the drive from Chicago to Miami took two weeks, three of those days within Florida itself. The railroads played a part, too: Seaboard Air Line extended its rails to Miami; the Atlantic Coast Line routed trains to Florida from the Midwest; and the Florida East Coast, Henry Flagler's original trail blazer, double-tracked its roadbed from Jacksonville to Miami. At the same time, Pensacola, long served by the Louisville and Nashville, gained access to the Midwest through a newcomer, the St. Louis and San Francisco.

In 1925, mainland property six and eight miles outside the city limits of Miami was commanding $25,999 an acre. It was hard for area residents to remember that on March 26, 1915, when Miami Beach was incorporated, Carl Fisher, one of its developers, had offered beach property free to anyone who would settle it. As housing subdivisions sprang up, hotels mushroomed, new stores opened, and money gained value daily in the stock market, there was a mounting constituency for developers who knew how to combine the stately architecture of Rome, the tiled rooftops of Spain, the dreamy beauty of Venice, the tropical casualness of Algiers—and call it "Mediterranean."

Bathing beauties at Miami Beach in May 1923. Such swimsuit photos, in the age well before Sports Illustrated, *were called "cheesecake." Receiving wide play in the nation's newspapers, they helped in attracting thousands to Miami Beach, which had been a vacant sandbar in 1915 but by 1925 boasted of 56 hotels with 4,000 rooms, 178 apartment buildings, three golf courses, four polo fields, and two churches. The new city, laid out along a purple-blue surf, was ornamented by imported coconut palm trees (like the one here), Australian pines, and sea lavender.*

A downtown Miami scene at the height of the boom in 1925. Barkers competed with automobile horns and drill hammers to announce the latest land bonanza. The Miami Daily News, *swollen by advertising columns, published an edition of 504 pages weighing seven and a half pounds, largest in newspaper history. Boosterism, now addictive, developed a dynamic that threatened all limits of reality and taste. Thoroughly carried away, the mayors of Miami, Miami Beach, Hialeah, and Coral Gables issued a joint proclamation declaring that their county was "the most Richly Blessed Community of the most Bountifully Endowed State of the most Highly Enterprising People of the Universe."*

Miamian George E. Merrick was one such developer. On November 27, 1921, he had sold the first lot in what would become Coral Gables. Merrick planned to fill 10,000 acres with pink and cream houses commingled with Spanish patios, wrought-iron balconies overhanging stone plazas, fountains, and streets named after Renaissance towns and kings. A coral rock quarry in the center of the development was fashioned into what Merrick called the Venetian Pool. There, on a concrete platform set over the water, no less a personage than William Jennings Bryan extolled the wondrous future of Merrick's city. It was the only city in the world, Bryan declared, "where you can tell a lie at breakfast that will come true by evening."

Seventy-five miles north, fantasy found another champion in the eccentric artisan-architect Addison Mizner of Palm Beach. With a commission from his friend, sewing machine heir Paris Singer, Mizner built the swank Everglades Club in 1918, after which he was importuned to accept commissions for house after house in his "bull market, damn-the-expense" Spanish style. What interior furnishings he could not scavenge from palaces and convents in Spain he produced in his own workshop, simulating worm holes in new wood by blasting it with shotguns. The final interior touches were doorknobs of solid gold, for, as he said, "It saves on the polishing." By the mid-twenties Mizner had created a pink-walled, red-tiled, wrought iron-gated world of unreal luxury, set amidst sea grapes, oleanders, and lofty coconut palms called Jamaica Talls. The railroad car set of tycoons and heiresses in oil, steel, gear boxes, and breakfast cereals was, at last, appropriately housed.

The Florida boom did not always make for such conspicuous splendor. In most places up and down the east coast and around Cape Sable to Fort Myers on the Gulf, as well as in the interior, developers had little to show but filled mangrove swamps or cleared pinelands, with rough-scraped dirt roads to outline subdivisions and stucco gateways announcing new towns-to-be. But in the land delirium of mid-decade even that much sold, and sold quickly, to northern "snowbirds."

Miami itself was bedlam. Flagler Street was jammed with shirt-sleeved men, their arms full of real estate forms,

A British visitor during the boom, Theyre Hamilton Weigall, recorded, "It was a common sight at any wayside barbecue on the Dixie Highway to see some purple-faced orator mounted on the back seat of his car under the blazing sun bellowing of the land of hope to an awestruck audience standing round him in the white dust." Often land was sold before it was dredged above the water level. These "predevelopment" sales were the occasion of numerous frauds. As Groucho Marx said in the movies, "You can get stucco. Oh, how you can get stucco!"

rushing from doorway to doorway, where barkers competed with automobile horns and drill hammers to announce the latest land bonanza. George Merrick alone had 3,000 salesmen in the streets. Chief of Police H. Leslie Quigg, desperate to control 300,000 people, recruited plowhands from Georgia, put them in uniforms, gave them revolvers, and sent them into the streets as policemen. One of them fired at a jaywalker.

Much of what was being sold was not land but paper. A 10 percent down payment would hold a property for thirty days. Paper profits rose to dizzying heights. "Hundreds" became "thousands," then "millions." Perspiring, fast-talking hucksters called "Binder Boys," in golf knickers and two-toned shoes, swapped paper so rapidly a single lot

Addison Mizner's first commissioned house on Palm Beach was El Mirasol, shown here, built for the Edward T. Stotesburys, of Philadelphia banking money. Mizner ad-libbed the design as he went, ending with thirty-seven rooms, a half dozen patios, an illuminated pool, and a forty-car underground garage. As an observer stated, it began looking like a convent and ended looking like a castle. Here the Stotesburys' daughter Louise married the young General Douglas MacArthur. Mrs. Stotesbury, "Queen Eva," reigned over Palm Beach society from the twenties through the thirties. When the Joshua Cosdens had Mizner build the seventy-room Playa Riente, Mrs. Stotesbury called Mizner back to enlarge her own competitive digs. Neither house stands today.

sometimes changed hands a dozen times a day. But by October 1925 the paper boom peaked. By February 1926 the *New York Times* reported a "lull." By July the *Nation* reported a "collapse": "The world's greatest poker game, played with building lots instead of chips, is over. And the players are now . . . paying up." The roads north became black with funeral-like corteges. Left behind were financial wreckage, unfinished buildings, garish swinging signs over empty streets, miles of cement sidewalks leading nowhere, jazz bands playing to empty halls, and broken dreams.

High society and old money preferred Palm Beach. This scene is on the beach side of the Breakers Hotel, where dress was as decorous as behavior. The nouveau riche preferred Miami, where illegal liquor parties in the hotels and clubs became showplaces for the new fashions and mores of the Roaring Twenties. Men wore white linen suits, eschewed cigars and chewing tobacco in favor of cigarettes, and sprinkled their conversation with "keen" and "nifty." The women wore straight, long-waisted dresses cut to boyish form and shortened daringly to above the knee, flattered their legs with flesh-colored silk or rayon stockings, bobbed or shingled their hair, openly used rouge and lipstick, and also smoked cigarettes—in holders.

The coup de grace was administered two months later by a fierce hurricane that slammed into the Gold Coast and Everglades with winds estimated to be between 130 and 150 miles an hour. Coming in the dead of night on September 18, 1926, the storm, the first since 1910, caught the new population unaware and unprepared. Its winds drove the ocean completely over Miami Beach and into downtown Miami. Ninety-two coastal residents were killed, and another 300 persons drowned at Moore Haven when a

The hurricane of September 18, 1926, that hit the Gold Coast and Everglades destroyed five thousand homes and damaged nine thousand more from Miami to Fort Lauderdale. The last remaining boom-time tent cities and tourist camps were leveled. Boats were blown inland and automobiles were washed out to sea. Boards were driven through trees, and railroad tracks were stood on edge like picket fences. As local folklore remembered it, "It blowed a crooked road straight, and scattered the days of the week so bad Sunday didn't get around 'til late Tuesday morning."

Lake Okeechobee dike crumbled and flooded the town. Over 6,000 were injured and 18,000 made homeless. The damage was immense. Two years later, almost to the day (September 16), another hurricane of equal strength hit the Florida shoreline at Palm Beach and dumped tons of water into Lake Okeechobee. The loss of life was estimated to be between 1,850 and 2,000 people, three-quarters of them black laborers—estimated because the bodies of many known to have lived in the region were never found.

As though these calamities were not chastisement enough for boom-time excesses, the citrus industry was staggered by a Mediterranean fruit fly infestation. First discovered on April 6, 1929, at Orlando, the infestation eventually reached 1,002 groves that accounted for 80 percent of state's citrus crop. The real estate collapse of 1926 had plunged Florida's economy into a deep depression, and no fewer than forty banks were forced to close in that year alone. Many reopened and other new banks started, but in 1929 dozens more failures occurred even before the national stock market crash on October 29 of that year. The state was an already prostrate victim of financial ruin when the ticker tape machines fell silent in New York City.

From that most colorful, tumultuous, and tragic of Florida's decades, there were some notable permanent results. The state's population increased by nearly half: from 968,470 in 1920 to 1,468,211 in 1930. Most of the increase was in the peninsula, where Jacksonville remained the largest city with 129,549, but Miami posted the most dramatic permanent growth, from 29,571 in 1920 to 110,637 by 1930. Tampa became third largest with 101,161 and St. Petersburg fourth with 40,425. In 1928 Miami and Tampa were joined by the 284-mile-long Tamiami Trail (U.S. 41) that, carved out of the solid rock that underlay the Everglades, featured the longest dike constructed outside of The Netherlands. (Environmentalists of a later generation would criticize the highway because it obstructed the flow of water and wildlife in the Big Cypress Swamp and the Everglades.) With most of the growth in the southern part of the state the decade saw the creation there of nine new counties: Charlotte, Glades, Hardee, Highlands, Sarasota, Collier, Hendry, Indian River, and Martin. Dixie, Union, Gilchrist, and Gulf counties were established in the northern section of the state. By 1930, it can safely be said, the frontier period was over and Florida was settled. Once pronouncedly agrarian, now becoming an urban state, it would be 1940 before 55 percent of its inhabitants would live in cities and towns.

Where social order was at issue, perhaps no greater progress was made during the period than in the state's abolition (in 1919 and 1923) of the convict lease system. For many years Florida had no penitentiary for the incarceration of convicts, and, following the pattern of other southern states, the state and counties leased prisoners to private contractors, such as operators of phosphate mines and turpentine camps. Many misuses and abuses had resulted, some of them highly publicized. Convict leasing with its lash and sweatbox did not end for good until 1923. After that date a prison farm at Raiford and convict road gangs replaced the older system.

Racism and Violence

Few of the material and social advances registered by the twenties touched the lives of Florida's African-American citizens, who, even after a migration of 40,000 to northern states in the period 1916–20, constituted 30 percent of the population and lived primarily in the backcountry, far from the land of the travel folders. There, bedeviled by white supremacy advocates, Jim Crow laws, capricious enforcement of vagrancy legislation, poor schools, if any, voting laws that barred them from the Democratic primaries, and a seemingly endless cycle of economic exploitation and impoverishment, blacks experienced life of a kind unimagined in the white coastal resorts, where about the only signs of prejudicial activity toward the few blacks in evidence were separate restrooms, drinking fountains, and other facilities for the "colored." Furthermore, blacks in the interior knew that at any time, for the slightest offense, real or imagined, they could be subject to physical violence, including death.

The lawless character of the hinterland, combined with the whites' racism, caused Florida to lead the country in lynchings, 4.5 per 10,000 blacks, twice the rates in Mississippi, Georgia, and Louisiana, three times the rate in Alabama, six times the rate in South Carolina. An entire black town could be obliterated on the slightest suggestion of wrongdoing, as happened at Rosewood (near Cedar Keys) in 1923 with, it is believed, six black people killed, including women and children; so could an entire black section of a town, as at Ocoee (near Orlando), with four deaths, three years before. In both cases, the entire populace fled.

At the Cuesta Rey factory in Ybor City in 1929, men and women cigarmakers silently rolled tobacco, mostly Cuban, into coronas, perfectos, and panatelas while el lector (the reader) on a raised platform (right) read to them from newspapers, tracts, and novels. The readers, who occupied an esteemed position in Cuban-American society, were paid directly by the workers, who also selected the material read, often Marxist or anarchist in character. Following a failed strike inspired by the Communist-backed Tobacco Workers International Union in 1931, the lectors were replaced by radios. The last surviving lector died in 1984.

Deep in the vast pine forests the turpentine camps subjected thousands of blacks to a more subtle violence, punctuated by beatings and killings, that carried the technical name peonage, a system more plainly described as forced labor. Although the state had outlawed convict leasing, another legislative act, in 1919, authorized turpentine operators to hold nonconvict workers for debt. Under this law an operator recruited black workers, and the company provided them transportation to the work site, placing them in debt for that service. The workers' annual bill for grits, pork, calico, and shoes always added up to more than his wages. The system, ensuring as it did that the blacks would never be out of debt, made quitting almost impossible. "You is *born* into the teppentime," one worker said, "Ain't nothing you *go* into. Something you get out *of.*" White riders wielding pistols and leather whips kept the blacks at constant work. The squalid forced labor and the overseers' justice in these pine pitch gulags would continue to stain the heart of Florida through the following decade, and in Alachua County until as late as 1949.

Tropical Depression

Presiding over Florida government as the state descended into the national collapse of 1929 was a newly elected governor, Doyle E. Carlton, native of Wauchula, Tampa attorney, and former state senator. He had won the chief state post in a year when the Florida vote for president went to a Republican for the first time in fifty-two years: Herbert C. Hoover defeated New York's Governor Alfred E. Smith 144,168 votes to 101,764. Alfred I. du Pont, heir to the E. I. du Pont de Nemours chemical fortune and newcomer to the state, pumped great sums into the Hoover campaign and boasted afterward, "I have made Florida Republican." Although the boast would not prove true, his brother-in-law and chief Florida aide, Edward "Mr. Ed" Ball, would exercise unprecedented control over state politics in north and west Florida for much of the next half century. In an interesting sideline to the 1928 balloting, incumbent Park Trammell, a former governor, defeated Governor John W. Martin in the race for U.S. senator, thus remaining the only former governor (and one of only three by 2003) to take the oath for a national elective office.

In Florida economic conditions worsened as both national and state banks failed in large numbers (113 would go under by 1932), property values dropped by a fourth, county and municipal bonds defaulted, the net income of corporations plummeted, winter tourist seasons failed to materialize, business people and farmers went bankrupt, and two railroads, the East Coast and the Seaboard, sank into receivership (in 1931). In Tampa, where pioneer radio station WDAE had advertised its call letters as standing for "Wonderful Days and Evenings," the announcers revised them to read "We Don't Always Eat." Florida was down and out. Voters blamed Hoover for the depression as vigorously as they had supported him four years earlier. In the elections of 1932, most turned to Democrat Franklin D. Roosevelt and his New Deal. A state candidate in the FDR mold, Daytona Beach attorney David Sholtz, won the second gubernatorial primary over former Governor Martin by the largest vote for that office in the state's history.

Relief and Recovery

Sholtz was able to leave office in 1936 with the state's financial and social condition markedly improved because the New Deal had pumped millions of federal dollars into Florida's stricken economy. The Civilian Conservation Corps (CCC) began a reforestation project at Eastport in Duval County in 1933; before it shut down in 1940, the CCC peaked at thirty-three work camps and gave employment to 40,000 young men under age twenty-five. Other agencies to replace the dole system with useful labor followed: the National Youth Administration (NYA), the Public Works Administration (PWA), the Federal Emergency Relief Administration (FERA), and, perhaps the most significant of all, beginning in 1935, the Works Progress Administration (WPA), which would employ 40,000 Floridians on public projects.

In an effort to siphon off the discontent of World War I veterans, many of whom had participated in the famous Bonus March on Washington in 1932, the Roosevelt admin-

Several months after his election, Governor David Sholtz greeted two other newly elected officials in Miami, President-elect Franklin D. Roosevelt and Mayor Anton Cermak of Chicago. On the evening of February 15, 1933, while Roosevelt and Mayor Cermak sat talking in an open car at crowded Bayfront Park, a would-be assassin named Giuseppe Zangara took aim at Roosevelt with a revolver. Two Miami citizens standing near Zangara, Mrs. Lillian Cross, wife of a physician, and Thomas Armour, a carpenter, grabbed for the gunman's arm. Their action saved his life, but because they were not able to deflect the gun upward, only sideways, the six shots Zangara managed to discharge wounded five persons in the crowd, Cermak among them. Here the mayor is shown being helped to a vehicle. The lone fatality, Cermak died nineteen days later from peritonitis. His killer pleaded guilty and was electrocuted at Raiford on March 20. The interval between the crime and the punishment was thirty-three days.

Newly elected Governor David Sholtz (center) is shown in 1933 at Jacksonville with President-elect Roosevelt (left) and Jacksonville Mayor John T. Alsop. Brooklyn-born Sholtz, who had moved to Daytona after naval service in World War I, won landslide victories in the 1932 second primary and general elections. He enthusiastically endorsed Roosevelt's New Deal. Thanks to such federal programs as FERA and WPA, Florida successfully rode out the depression, and, in one notable example, Key West was saved from bankruptcy and ruin. So plentiful were the federal dollars, Sholtz built a bridge across Ochlockonee Bay at Panacea in the Panhandle, though there was no existing road to join it. Years later, a road, now U.S. 98, was built to serve the bridge.

istration sent 684 men to work in three CCC camps on Windley and Matecumbe keys between the mainland and Key West. Their task was to construct an overseas causeway for automobiles in parallel with Henry Flagler's Overseas Railroad. On Labor Day, September 2, 1935, the strongest hurricane ever recorded, with winds at 200 miles per hour, roared across the Keys and took 408 lives, most of them veterans. The calamity was compounded when all the cars of a rescue train were blown off the tracks by the fierce winds.

By the winter of 1935–36, the flow of tourists into the state had picked up somewhat. As a result of their spending, economic stability would return to Florida more quickly than it did to other states in the South. And the tourists were now of many different kinds: the still wealthy with their winter homes; the nightclubbing excursionists on Miami Beach; the working families who "went to the beach" or visited the inland lakes and attractions; the compulsive motorists in new $515 Ford V-8s or Chrysler Airflows who cruised the state's 3,500 miles of highway; the elderly who leased seaside cottages and played shuffleboard; and so-called Tin Can Tourists of the World, who lived in campers or tents and migrated in groups through the central and Gulf Coast counties. (Of the tin canners, a future governor, Fuller Warren, said, unkindly, "They came to Florida with one suit of underwear and one twenty dollar bill, and changed neither.") Another type of tourist, even less desirable to Floridians, was indigent transients, not only single drifters but desperate families as well, who poured into Florida looking for work and warmth. For three winter seasons state police took the extreme step of patrolling highway entrances to the state and turning back travelers who lacked provable means of support—an estimated 50,000 in the winter of 1935–36.

When fourteen candidates qualified for the Democratic nomination for governor in 1936, the largest number ever, it was said that the times were so hard that men ran for governor in order to make a living. A more serious commentator would have called attention to the traditionally factional political system which on the surface made Florida resemble less a one-party or a two-party state than it did a multiparty state in the European model. Florida was too large geographically, its various populations too dispersed and too dissimilar in cultures, economic interests, and ethnic groupings to expect, even in an overwhelmingly Democratic state, that political loyalties could avoid the same fragmentation. Most candidates for governor started out with local rather than with statewide followings. Any individual with money enough for a filing fee and some political standing in his own county could announce as a candidate in the first primary for governor. If he was lucky enough to win strongly in home and adjacent counties and something like 20 percent of the vote elsewhere, he could find himself in the second primary.

That is what happened to Fred Cone, Lake City banker and long-time figure in the Democratic party. With an appealing campaign promise to "lower the budget to balance taxes instead of raising taxes to balance the budget," Old Suwannee, as he was known to his Cracker friends, easily won the Democratic runoff that was tantamount to election. Cone called the growth in state government "astounding and rotten," yet he did not turn down millions in federal assistance. His vetoes of 154 bills were three times more than any previous governor's. The most positive accomplishments of Cone's administration were in the tax structure. The poll tax as a prerequisite to voting and state taxes on land were abolished, and the first homestead exemptions were allowed. By increasing excise taxes on cigarettes, intoxicating beverages, automobiles, and gasoline, Florida shifted the burden of taxation to consumers and users of manufactured products.

During his second year in office Cone suffered a double coronary occlusion. Thereafter, he was frequently incapacitated and many executive decisions were made independently by his longtime secretary from White Springs, Ella Neill. Like Woodrow Wilson's wife, Edith Bolling Galt, in the last eighteen months of her stricken husband's presidency, Miss Ella, as everyone called her, veritably ruled without reigning. For all practical purposes, over much of two years' time, Ella Neill was the first woman governor of Florida. To her office by day, and to her apartment by night, came key state employees, city officials, lobbyists, and citizen-petitioners. From her rendering of Cone's signature went out appointments (including that of a circuit judge), dismissals, and a multiplicity of official documents. Nor did she count commutations of the death sentence outside her powers. When in 1940 Cone recovered sufficiently to retake the reins of government, he fired Miss Ella.

By the 1930s only three Florida women had gained election to major public offices: Ruth Bryan Owen, daughter of William Jennings Bryan and a resident of Miami, who served two terms beginning in 1928 as the state's first congresswoman; Edna Giles Fuller of Orange County, who was elected to the state House, also in 1928; and Mamie Eaton Greene of Monticello, who in the same year won election to the state Railroad Commission (a post to which she had been appointed the previous year to complete the unexpired term of her husband). Fourteen years would pass before another woman would be elected to statewide office.

An exciting new face appeared on the political scene in 1936, Tallahassee attorney Claude Denson Pepper. A native of Alabama with a Harvard law degree, Pepper had come to Perry in 1925 and had won election to the Florida legislature as a representative of Taylor County in 1929. He lost his seat two years later, in part because he voted against a legislative resolution that condemned Mrs. Herbert Hoover for having invited a black person to tea. For the next six years he served in numerous state and Democratic party capacities, all the while making friends with politicians and business people and displaying his awesome oratorical skills on ceremonial occasions. By 1936 when he announced for U.S. senator (replacing Duncan Fletcher, who died that year), he was unbeatable.

In Washington, Pepper identified himself completely with Roosevelt and the New Deal, thus providing an interesting counterpoint to Cone's conservatism and giving heart to Florida's still significant numbers of unemployed and underpaid laborers. In the senatorial elections of 1938, Pepper had to face charges that he had "bought" votes by arranging to have 5,600 people added to the relief rolls. He need not have worried. In a vote that was widely interpreted as a ratification of the New Deal in Florida, Pepper overwhelmed four candidates to win in the first primary. His campaign manager at the University of Florida was a young law student named George Smathers. As reward for his help, Pepper arranged for Smathers to be appointed assistant district attorney in Miami. The popular Smathers, for his part, promised never to run against his benefactor—a promise he kept until 1950, when Ed Ball came calling, and Florida recoiled before the most vitriolic campaign in its history.

Industry and Agriculture

As Florida entered the 1940s, its industry and agriculture, slower than tourism to recover from the depression, were demonstrating new vitality and on a wider base than before. Production of paper from slash pine had become commercially competitive during the thirties, and the International Paper Company, followed shortly by the du Pont interests (St. Joe Paper Company), opened pulp mills at Panama City and Port St. Joe, respectively, to take advantage of the millions of acres of Panhandle pinelands. Virgin timber was rapidly being depleted, however. Because of fires, indiscriminate cutting, and failure to reseed, Florida possessed only one-fourth of its original area of forest land—and the New Deal reforestation programs were vigorously pushed.

At Tarpon Springs, Greek-Americans in diving suits worked the Gulf's sponge beds. Cigar making, moved from Key West to east Tampa in the last century by Vicente Martinez Ybor, was thriving. Ybor City's 122 factories employed 10,000 workers. With filler tobacco from Cuba and wrapper leaf from this country, the cigar makers, three men to a team, sat at long benches and hand-rolled over 250 million coronas, royals, perfectos, and panatelas a year. An entirely mechanized factory at Jacksonville, employing two thousand workers, mostly young white women, was able to double Tampa's production—a sign of things to come, in Florida and elsewhere.

The living conditions of migrant farmers and packers in Florida were hard at any time, but doubly so during the Great Depression. For many they were "root hog-or-die" times. The luckier fruit and vegetable workers lived in wooden cabins, "single 2 dollars a week, double 4 dollars, water must be hauled." Others, like this Tennessee family at a Winter Haven packing house, camped in their car: "We never lived like hogs before, but we sure does now." Watch out with those scissors, young fella!

These strawberry "processors" at a Plant City packinghouse paused for a photograph on May 16, 1935. Labor unions were not popular in Florida (or in the rest of the South), but by the mid-thirties unions had been formed among fruit and vegetable pickers and packers, railroad porters, streetcar employees, telegraphers, cigarmakers, pulp and paper workers, longshoremen and dockers, shipyard workers, the building trades, and typesetters. Numerous strikes occurred, with varying results. At Lake Alfred and Winter Haven in 1938 citrus growers and packing plant operators, faced with a glutted fruit market, closed their operations rather than give workers a raise. By the 1940s unions claimed 20 percent of Florida's stable work force.

All the cars of this rescue train, sent to remove World War I veteran-laborers from the path of a Labor Day hurricane in the Keys in 1935, were blown off the tracks by the fierce winds, the highest ever recorded on the Atlantic coast. A total of 408 persons, most of them veterans, were killed. So damaged by the storm were the rails and trestles of Flagler's line that the bankrupt Florida East Coast Railway Company sold its right-of-way and roadbed for use as an overseas automobile highway, which opened in 1938.

Phosphate, first discovered on the Peace River near Arcadia in 1884, showed promise of becoming the large industry that it was by the 1970s. Citrus packing and canning houses multiplied; they not only handled oranges and grapefruit for shipment, but workers canned or bottled juices, candied and crystallized peels, and made marmalades and jellies. Large-scale production of raw sugar from Everglades cane was under way at Clewiston on the southern shore of Lake Okeechobee, where the United States Sugar Corporation had established a pioneer processing mill in 1929. Seaboard and the Atlantic Coast Line,

Governor Fred P. Cone (left) *shown with Senator Claude Pepper in the late 1930s. The two men could not have been less alike politically. Cone's administration was probably the most fiscally conservative of the century. Pepper was one of the nation's leading advocates of President Roosevelt's New Deal. Cone, who had campaigned on a platform of "cutting the budget to the bone and then scraping the bone," had no taste for the deficit spending that fueled the New Deal, though he willingly benefited from its programs. His most criticized decision was a refusal to provide the matching state funds required to obtain federal grants to build or improve buildings at state institutions. When World War II created vast demands for buildings, the state would be handicapped in meeting them.*

together with Florida's own reviving East Coast Line, extended their rails, and Seaboard, using what it declared to be the most powerful diesel electric locomotives in the world, ran the first New York-Miami chair coach streamline train, the Silver Meteor. Air traffic also showed impressive gains: by the forties there were three scheduled air carriers in the state, Pan American, Eastern, and a Florida corporation founded in St. Petersburg, National Airlines, Inc.

In agriculture, Florida was relatively free of the twin evils of farm tenancy and the one-crop system. Seventy percent of white farmers and 53 percent of black farmers owned their own farms. Variations in climate and soil divided the state into four distinct agricultural regions: southern, where winter vegetables and sugarcane grew in the reclaimed Everglades mucklands (the region produced one of every five teaspoons of sugar consumed in the U.S.); central, where the highest concentration of citrus in the world thrived on the sandy loam hills and in the river valleys; northern, where general farming was the rule; and western, or Panhandle, where corn was the principal staple. Florida had been one of the first cattle-raising regions of the country, from the days when Spanish cattle barons ranched the Alachua country. By the start of the forties it was becoming a leading beef cattle producer. A strong tradition of open ranges still resisted the demand of citizens, mainly automobile owners, for state-enforced fencing, which would not come until 1949 and 1952.

Few Florida industries, including agribusiness, provided year-round work to the resident population, and most unskilled labor such as crop pickers and hotel help was migrant or transient. Skilled labor with steady employment increasingly moved toward organization under the national auspices of the CIO or the AFL. Twenty percent of Florida's stable work force, or 4 percent of the total population, was unionized by 1940. Unions were not popular in the South generally, and Florida was no exception. Union members entered the 1940s heartened by the creation of a Florida industrial commission and a state welfare board, as well as by passage of a workmen's compensation law.

World War II

Although a seat in the U.S. Senate was his long-term goal, and he considered the governor's office a political graveyard ("If you appoint a man to office, you make one ingrate

Tens of thousands of construction workers poured into tiny Starke in 1940 and 1941 to work at nearby Camp Blanding. Their living accommodations may have been rude and bare, as shown here, but columnist Ward Morehouse of the New York Sun *described Starke itself, with fourteen times its normal population, as "an overnight goldrush town . . . neoned and streamlined . . . as fantastic a spot as America now presents . . . with its overlighted facades, its blazing interiors, its fluorescent tubing, its while-U-wait photo studios, its hell-red neons, its cheap jewelry displays and its gaudy movie palaces."*

and ten enemies"), Bartow-born Spessard L. Holland was nonetheless persuaded to run for governor in the primaries of 1940, and he won the runoff with 57 percent of the vote. Holland was inaugurated in January 1941, eleven months before the Japanese attack on Pearl Harbor, which would plunge the United States into the world war already raging in Europe and Asia.

In November 1940, the Florida National Guard was mobilized to active duty. Early in 1941, the first of a long line of

In 1941, Marion Post, a famed Farm Security Administration photographer, captured the mood of black male Floridians in a South Florida juke joint and bar. Black social life did not extend to Florida's beaches at the time, except at a handful of sites, such as the Colored Section of Ben T. Davis Beach off the causeway between Tampa and Clearwater, American Beach at Fernandina, Butler's Beach below St. Augustine, and the Colored Only beach at Virginia Key, Miami. In public places the seating areas, restrooms, and drinking fountains were marked "white" and "colored." While blacks of college age could enroll at the Florida Agricultural and Mechanical College in Tallahassee during the 1940s, they were denied admittance to the state-supported University of Florida in Gainesville and the Florida State College for Women (later Florida State University) in Tallahassee, as well as the private University of Miami.

During 1942–43 Miami Beach took on the appearance of an armed camp, where five acres of servicemen in gas masks did calisthenics, long columns of uniformed trainees marched along streets, parks, and golf courses, and an alert movie fan could catch sight of Clark Gable, William Holden, or Robert Preston in close order drill. The Army Air Forces alone occupied seventy thousand hotel rooms on the beach, where one-fourth of all air officers and one-fifth of all air enlisted men received basic training. Hotel space opened up to tourists again in late 1943 when most trainees had shipped overseas.

British Royal Air Force cadets arrived in Florida to take flight training at Dorr and Carlstrom fields in Arcadia. The Naval Air Station at Pensacola, first opened in 1914, underwent its eighth expansion. A second Naval Air Station, with later auxiliary bases at Mayport and Green Cove Springs, began operations at Jacksonville. A new southeastern regional Army Air Forces base at Tampa was named to honor an Illinois native, Colonel Leslie MacDill, killed in the crash of his plane at Bolling Field, Virginia in 1938. It was later joined at Tampa by Drew and Henderson fields. An army air proving ground, named after another military crash victim, Lieutenant Colonel Frederick J. Eglin (who died in 1937), was activated at Valparaiso in the Panhandle. Soon to be famous as the site where Lieutenant Colonel James H. Doolittle trained his B-25 bomber pilots for the carrier-launched raid on Tokyo in 1942, Eglin forty years afterward would be the largest air force base in the Western world. Other air training facilities, army and navy, sprang up at Sebring, Fort Myers, Lakeland, Avon Park, Sanford, Banana River, Vero Beach, Fort Lauderdale, Miami, and elsewhere, with the result that Florida, with its good year-round flying weather and level, sparsely occupied terrain, bristled with forty active military fields by war's end. Tragically, hundreds of pilots were killed in Florida training accidents, many more, it is estimated, than the 507 RAF pilots who were lost in the Battle of Britain.

At Kingsley Lake eight miles east of Starke, the army built a basic training camp in honor of retired Major General Albert H. Blanding, a graduate of Gainesville's East Florida Seminary who became head of the Florida National Guard and went on to head the National Guard Bureau at Washington in the 1930s. At its peak—90,000 enlistees and draftees under training in 125,000 acres of scrub oak thickets—Camp Blanding was the fourth largest city in Florida. Filled with imported construction workers, Starke, formerly a quiet strawberry center, became a neon-lit boom town. Meanwhile, welders from across the country poured into Florida to build cargo ships at Jacksonville and Tampa shipyards.

Any illusions that the war was remote were broken when, ten weeks after Pearl Harbor, a German submarine, U-*128*, entered the congested shipping lanes twenty miles off Cape Canaveral in the Florida Straits and on the night of February 19, 1942, torpedoed and sank the U.S. tanker *Pan Massachusetts*. The stricken vessel's cargo of gasoline and fuel oil exploded into towering flames that woke and frightened thousands of beach and intracoastal waterway residents. So it continued into the summer: from Fernandina Beach to the Keys and around into the Gulf, one after another tanker or merchantman, defenseless against the prowling German seawolves, sank in flames before the helpless gaze of Floridians on their beach-cottage decks and tourists on their hotel balconies. At Jacksonville Beach on the evening of April 10, revelers at the amusement park were shocked to see and hear the violent red explosion of a loaded tanker, the SS *Gulfamerica*, just four miles offshore. When the fiery hulk refused to sink, its assailant, U-*123*, came between the beach and the tanker to ventilate the waterline with a deck gun. U-boat commander Kapitänleutnant Reinhard Hardegen wrote in his report of the sinking: "A burning tanker, artillery fire, the silhouette of a U-boat—how often had all of that been seen in America?"

In the pre-dawn hours of June 17, 1942, a German U-boat, U-*584*, deposited four saboteurs on the beach four miles south of Ponte Vedra, a small resort community south of Jacksonville Beach. They were supplied with American-made clothing, $70,000 in U.S. currency, forged documents, and four large wooden waterproof boxes filled with explosives of various kinds. On landing they buried their equipment for later retrieval and walked north along the beach. In Jacksonville two of them registered at the Mayflower Hotel, the other two at the Seminole Hotel. Unknown to them, the leader of a similar Nazi landing party in Long Island had turned informer, and they were under constant surveillance by the FBI. The four saboteurs who landed in Florida, along with two from the northern group, were electrocuted by the army on August 8, 1942, in Washington, D.C.

Thousands of civilian volunteers, men and women called "spotters," kept track of all air activity in observation posts and information centers on Florida's coastlines. Over 250,000 Florida citizens were organized to serve in other capacities, such as air raid wardens, dimout monitors, auxiliary firemen, or nurses' aides, and just about everyone, including children, collected paper, scrap metal, and grease for the war effort. Most citizens of driving age had "A" stickers, which allowed access to three gallons of gasoline a week.

Nearly 3,000 German prisoners, beginning with U-boat captives in 1942 and Wehrmacht veterans of General Erwin Rommel's Afrika Korps in 1943, worked in 15 labor camps throughout Florida helping to harvest citrus and other perishable crops, to can fruits and vegetables, and to cut lumber. POWs from the Kendall camp in Dade County were put to work cleaning streets in Miami Beach, where women pedestrians on Alton Road complained of being whistled at, and one used her handbag as part of the war effort.

Although the tourist industry on which Florida depended for 60 percent of its income collapsed in the first year of the war because of dimouts, oil-filled beaches, gasoline shortages, and military call-ups, the federal government compensated for many of the losses through the payrolls and other support given to military installations of all kinds that dotted the landscape from Pensacola to Key West, and through the leasing of 500 resort hotels in Miami Beach and elsewhere for use as military barracks, schools, hospitals, or convalescent centers. The Air Forces alone occupied 70,000 hotel rooms on Miami Beach. The Coast Guard trained at Flagler's Ponce de Leon Hotel in St. Augustine. Hotels in other cities hosted servicewomen— WACs, WAAFs, and WAVEs. Tourists would regain ascendancy in the resort areas by the summer of 1943, when military forces moved overseas, leaving half of the leased hotels vacant. With the end of the war in August 1945, Florida readied itself for the most explosive and enduring prosperity in its long history.

Returning home were not only the 250,000 men (including three Seminole Indians) and women that Florida had sent off to the armed forces but also tens of thousands of the 2,122,100 men and women from other states who had trained in Florida, together with their sweethearts, wives, and families who had followed them and liked what they had seen. They came this time as tourists, and many remained to make Florida their domicile. Veterans Administration financing made possible the construction of new

*The German submarine U-123 sank three ships in Florida waters in April 1942:
the tanker* Gulfamerica, *off Jacksonville Beach, and two freighters,* Leslie *and*
Korsholm, *off Cape Canaveral. Its commander, Kapitänleutnant Reinhard
Hardegen, is shown here (center) on the conning tower bridge, flanked by his
first and second watch officers, Rudolf Hoffmann (left) and Horst von Schroeter
(right). Hardegen, who earlier led "Operation Drumbeat," Germany's first military attack against the United States in World War II, is alive in Bremen at the
date of this writing. Von Schroeter, also alive, in Bonn, rose to the highest rank,
that of vice-admiral, in the postwar German fleet in NATO. Hoffmann also sur-
vives. This photo was taken in 1942 while their U-boat was operating off the
U.S. coast. U-boats sank over two dozen ships in Florida waters from January to
August 1942.*

During the war Florida's skies were filled with aircraft such as these P-39 Airacobra fighters at Ft. Myers, practicing single or close formation flying. At Opa-locka the Navy flew TBF torpedo bombers, which carried a pilot and crewman gunner. One day in 1943, while flying in formation, the propeller of one TBF accidentally cut off the tail of the plane ahead of it. The pilot of the stricken plane yelled into his microphone, which was on transmission at the time instead of intercom, "Pilot to crew! Bail out!" Aircraft all over South Florida heard the message, and 108 crewmen hit the silk in the southern counties.

homes, and postwar advances in mosquito control, air conditioning, and electric refrigeration improved the quality of daily life. (No complaint about Florida life, from mission days to the 1940s, had been more persistent or vocal than the complaint about mosquitoes, although one should not overlook cockroaches, ants, chiggers, yellow flies, gnats, no-see'ems, jellyfish, sandburs, beggarweed, and pine pollen.) From that date forward Florida would move steadily up the list in national population rank and would experience all the economic benefits—and all the social problems and environmental dislocations—that rapid growth can bring. In the forties the country's population as a whole would grow 15 percent but Florida's a startling 46 percent.

Postwar Politics

For Spessard Holland the governorship did not turn out to be the graveyard he had expected. When U.S. Senator Charles O. Andrews, Sr., announced that he would not seek reelection in 1946, Holland easily won that year's primary and general election to become only the second former governor (Park Trammell being the other) to take the oath after election to such an office. (Napoleon Broward had won election to the U.S. Senate in 1910 but died before assuming office.)

Succeeding Holland as governor was Millard Fillmore Caldwell, native of Tennessee and resident of Milton since 1924. Caldwell had served in the Florida house (1929–31) and in Congress (1933–41). He was cast in the same morally upright and decorous mold as Holland, a frequent political ally. Principal among the problems he faced were the exercise of effective leadership of the elected cabinet and the appointment of qualified people to the "little cabinet." Florida is unique among the states in that its elected cabinet acts collegially as a governing board for a variety of state agencies and responsibilities. Caldwell, with just one vote, could not dominate his cabinet and its decisions. His leadership had to be one of persuasion, at which he proved to be very good. The little cabinet, composed of the heads of a myriad of commissions, boards, and funds, was impervious to direction. Caldwell managed that problem by conscientiously selecting, with the help of trusted friends across the state, the most capable individuals he could find to serve as appointees.

His one term (the constitution would not allow two until a revision in 1968) is best remembered for bringing about passage of the Minimum Foundation Program for public schools, a landmark joint state-county funding mechanism that provided a "floor" of minimum funding for every school district in the state, thus bridging the gap between educational services offered in the wealthiest and the poorest counties. The MFP, as it came to be called, was first proposed in 1947 by a Citizens' Committee on Education which, acknowledging Florida's standing as forty-sixth among the states in the quality of its schools and teachers, argued that "money expended on schools may yield greater returns in dollars and cents than money spent in any single industry or other type of economic activity." The MFP was not altogether forward-looking: one of its purposes was to prevent federal courts from finding black schools to be unequal.

Caldwell established a standard of professionalism by which every subsequent governor would be judged. All too quickly that standard would be challenged by a man who had trained himself from youth to be governor and, when he finally got there, proved to have more style than substance. Born in the rural Panhandle town of Blountstown, Fuller Warren had studied at the University of Florida. In 1926, at twenty years of age and still a college senior, he parlayed his campus political experience into a successful race for the state house seat from his native Calhoun County. After one term, less than successful because of his age and inexperience, he studied law and, in 1929, opened a law practice in Jacksonville. In 1948 his flamboyant oratory drowned out the more measured voice of Caldwell-backed gubernatorial candidate Daniel T. McCarty, Fort Pierce citrus grower and cattleman, in a second primary campaign that turned more on personalities than it did on issues. The result was a Warren victory in a November election that was also notable for the fact that many conservative Florida Democrats deserted their party to vote for "Dixiecrat" Governor Strom Thurmond (S.C.) for president.

Like Catts in 1917–21, Fuller Warren was more interesting for the campaign he ran than for what he did in office. If his administration has a place at all in the popular memory, it is for the fact that Warren was the governor who finally took the cattle off the highways, pushing through an effective

Fuller Warren displaying his charm during the 1948 campaign for governor. No governor in modern times has matched his charismatic personality and gift for oratory. "I recommend the use of many adjectives," he said, "in fact a profusion, a plethora of adjectives. The goal of most orators is sound, not sense, and an array of euphonious, alliterative adjectives makes mightily for sound." Warren won the governor's race, but to most Floridians his administration made neither sound nor sense, and he

fencing bill for state roads in one year and for county roads two years later. All his life he wanted to be governor, but acting like one was not to his taste. "I must confess that I almost overmatched myself when I got hold of this governorship," he candidly told the *Miami Herald* in 1950. "It has been the roughest, toughest, most terrifying task I ever confronted." Reluctantly, he violated an inaugural pledge and supported the institution of a limited sales tax—3 percent, highest in the nation at the time. Many merchants said sarcastically, "For Fuller," as they dropped pennies into the tax box. Warren's capability as governor was impaired by charges that he was the tool of three heavy contributors to a contributor and aides, with organized crime. He survived an impeachment vote in the house, but from May 1951 until the end of his term, he effectively removed himself from office, spending almost all his time on the road, in the state and across the country, doing what he did best, selling Florida as a place to live and do business. There, on the hustings, he was at home, scattering adjectives in his booming voice and taking pleasure from the thrilled response of the crowds. When finally he stepped down from the office that had been his life's ambition, he could look back on several progressive and courageous initiatives on behalf of blacks and women that, in their way, were more significant than his many failures. Advisors and friends may have profited from government, but Warren remained incorruptible. He departed Tallahassee in 1953 with less means probably than any governor in the century and was insolvent when he died in a Miami hotel apartment in 1973.

Taking Stock Culturally

By midcentury Florida had come of age in a number of cultural forms, particularly in the historical and literary arts. Historians flourished during the fifty-year period, among whom one may name Caroline Mays Brevard, William Watson Davis, T. Frederick Davis, Jeannette Thurber Connor, Corita Doggett Corse, Rembert W. Patrick, and the Hannas, Alfred Jackson and Kathryn Abbey. Ernest Hemingway was the best known literary artist, and his stucco house on Whitehead Street in Key West was listed in the local guidebook as a point of interest for tourists. Only one novel with a Florida theme developed from his years in residence, *To Have and Have Not* (1937), and by critical consensus it was not his most successful effort. "Papa" Hemingway was not the only literary figure, or the most representative, to whom the state could lay claim, directly or indirectly. At work on Florida subjects in the thirties and forties were Stephen Vincent Benét, Edwin Granberry,

MacKinlay Kantor, Theodore Pratt, Edith Pope, Frank Slaughter, Marjory Stoneman Douglas, Philip Wylie, James Branch Cabell, Zora Neale Hurston, and Marjorie Kinnan Rawlings.

If there was one writer who by midcentury was identified by the nation's readers as being a Florida writer, it was Rawlings, who left her newspaper job in Rochester in 1928 to take up residence in the sparsely settled scrub at Cross Creek between Gainesville and Ocala. There, in the virgin stillness and beauty of Florida's interior, she cultivated orange trees and tried her hand at fiction, taking as her subjects the proud, taciturn Crackers who eked out a marginal existence from the fields, woods, and lakes. In these people Rawlings found unusual kindliness, spirituality, and nobility. Rawlings's approach to these pioneer inhabitants of what she called "the invisible Florida" was as objective as it was sympathetic, and she depicted their lives, together with the elemental beauty and danger of their surroundings, in a series of novels, notably a Pulitzer Prize winner, *The Yearling* (1938). In retrospect, *Cross Creek* (1942), an autobiographical reverie about her years among the creek people, stands forth as her masterful achievement.

Architecture was another field in which Florida had a distinguished tradition, one that extended from John M. Carrère and Thomas W. Hastings, who designed the Ponce de Leon Hotel in St. Augustine and Henry Flagler's mansion "Whitehall" in Palm Beach, to Henry John Klutho's "Chicago School" designs in Jacksonville after the turn of the century, to Mizner at Palm Beach, and to Frank Lloyd Wright, who by 1950 had designed four buildings on the campus of Florida Southern College, in Lakeland, and would design three more in the decade that followed. Nowhere by midcentury was the diversity of Florida's architectural styles more evident than in Dade County, where "bungalow," "mission," "depression moderne," and "streamline moderne massing," or "Art Deco," predominated. The Art Deco hotels and apartment houses in Miami Beach constituted then, and still do, the largest concentration of that style anywhere in the United States. The James Deering estate (built 1913) on Biscayne Bay provided an example of Italian Renaissance extravagance.

Ernest Hemingway's home at 907 Whitehead Street in Key West. Here in 1937 the novelist wrote his only book with a Florida theme, To Have and Have Not. *The two-story masonry house with stucco finish and verandas on all sides at both floors was built in 1851 by Asa Forsyth Tift, a local shipping merchant, who quarried coral rock at the site for the building's foundation and made the quarry hole a basement. Hemingway purchased the house in 1935. Today it is a museum. Since "Papa" Hemingway's time Key West has become a major literary colony, home to many of the nation's leading novelists, poets, and dramatists.*

The home of Marjorie Kinnan Rawlings at Cross Creek, where the novelist wrote several novels, including her Pulitzer Prize winner, The Yearling *(1938). Her autobiographical* Cross Creek *(1942) drew a $100,000 lawsuit from one of the characters described in the book, spinster Zelda Cason, an Island Grove social worker. Though required by the state supreme court to pay only token damages of one dollar and costs, Rawlings vowed never to write about Florida again. Her attorney, Philip S. May, of Jacksonville, attempted to dissuade her: "Ponce de León discovered Florida in 1512," he wrote her, " but he had found only the physical and material Florida. Then, more than 400 years later, you came to discover the heart and spirit of Florida and revealed them to the world in writings of rare beauty and sensitiveness." Rawlings, having kept her vow, died in 1953 at age fifty-seven.*

Jacksonville native James Weldon Johnson (1874–1938) was a poet, essayist, educator, journalist, song writer, diplomat, and lawyer. In 1900 he collaborated with his musician brother J. Rosamond to compose the inspirational song "Lift Every Voice and Sing," which the NAACP adopted as the Negro national anthem. Three of his books achieved wide notice: Autobiography of an Ex-Colored Man *(1937), about a close friend;* God's Trombones: Seven Negro Sermons in Verse; *(1927); and* Negro Americans, What Now? *(1934), which sought solutions for black-white problems in America.*

Zora Neale Hurston, born in the all-black town of Eatonville, near Orlando, was a distinguished folklorist, novelist, and anthropologist. In Mules and Men *(1935) she described black folk life, which also became a theme of fifty short stories and four novels, notably* Their Eyes Were Watching God *(1937) and* Dust Tracks on a Road *(1942). A leading member of the Harlem Renaissance group of writers and dramatists in the 1930s, she spent her last years in poverty and obscurity as a domestic servant in Fort Pierce, where in 1960 she was buried in an unmarked grave. Her reputation rescued in 1978 by anthropologists, she has enjoyed more fame in death than she did in life.*

Florida at Midcentury

By 1950 Florida's population reached 2,771,305, which placed it twentieth among the states and next among South Atlantic states after Virginia, North Carolina, and Georgia. During the first half of the century, Florida's growth rate in every decade had exceeded the national average. Sixty-five percent of Floridians lived in urban areas, and nearly one-half of the state's people lived in the metropolitan districts of only five cities: Miami (by this date the largest), Jacksonville, Tampa, St. Petersburg, and Orlando. One benefit of the growing urbanism of Florida was a developing benign attitude toward blacks in the larger cities. Urbanization tended to discourage racist demagoguery and "Negro-baiting." Not until the sixties would the benignity of urban whites be tested by an aggressive black drive for full equality.

The growth of the cities, some like Jacksonville and Miami, as far apart as 350 miles, accentuated a sociopolitical problem endemic to the state. So large were Florida's geographic dimensions—the road distance from Key West to Pensacola, for example, was nearly that from Pensacola to Chicago—and so diverse the populations and interests in the cities and the rural areas, that politicians and others bent on fusing Florida's people into a social whole found it difficult to overcome the entrenched economic differences and political localism. Not until 1956 would a candidate for state office succeed in putting together a coalition that embraced all the cities. The Johns Hopkins University political scientist, V. O. Key, Jr., writing in 1949, pinpointed the problem by superimposing a map of Florida on a map of the United States with Jacksonville positioned over Lansing, Michigan. The result showed that unifying Floridians into a common citizenry was akin to unifying the inhabitants of Lansing, Michigan, Dubuque, Iowa, Muncie, Indiana, and Huntington, West Virginia.

At midcentury tourism held a slight lead over agriculture as the state's leading revenue producer. Taking full advantage of Florida's geographical location, its sunshine and climate, miles of wide beaches, interior scenic attractions, and popularly priced automobiles, the travel and recreation industries enjoyed what has been called the 1950 boom. Almost a million automobiles crossed into Florida that year for recreational purposes. In the same year 45 percent of the total of 4.5 million tourists arrived by train, bus, or airplane. Awaiting these dollar-laden visitors was a tourist industry that included not only hotels, residential rentals, tourist courts, and motels—"Ocean Breeze," "Sand and Sea," "Sunrise Inn"—restaurants, bars, commercial attractions, racetracks, and jai-alai frontons, but also gas stations, food stores, dry goods and gift stores, and a myriad of suppliers and service personnel. While the winter season from January to April attracted the largest number of visitors, the summer months were starting to bring significant numbers of two-week vacationers, by car, from nearby southern states.

Dramatic improvements in the state road system were needed to improve traffic flow, and between 1949 and 1953 the state invested $500 million to rebuild and rehabilitate 3,000 miles of primary and secondary roads and bridges, a sum that represented nearly one-third of the total amount expended on highways since the State Road Department was established in 1915. A forty-five-mile Jacksonville Expressway, costing $60 million, sped cars and trucks through that city, the first sections opening in 1953. In the following year the Sunshine Skyway Bridge across Tampa Bay trimmed forty miles off the distance between St. Petersburg and Bradenton. Funds were appropriated for the four-laning of U.S. 1 from the Georgia line to Homestead (below Miami) and for a new high-speed, limited access toll turnpike to carry traffic along a 265-mile north-south artery between Wildwood (south of Ocala) and Miami. Both projects were completed in 1964, and the toll road, first called the Sunshine State Parkway, later Florida's Turnpike, would be a success from the start, in the return made on construction bonds and in the rapid, convenient service it provided automobile traffic to tourist meccas in the South. The next major improvement would come with the interstate highway system.

Florida's second-ranked industry, agriculture, enjoyed similar prosperity in 1950. Most farmers, white and black, owned the farms they managed. There was growing

Oranges and grapefruit thrived on the sandy loam hills and river valleys of Central Florida. Oranges were shipped out individually wrapped in wax paper, as these products of Lake Weir. The sign on the shipping box proclaimed, "You don't know oranges until you try our Banner Brand." A method of evaporating most of the water from orange juice, then freezing the residue and canning it, was developed in 1943–44 by Florida citrus researchers Dr. L. G. MacDowell and Dr. A. L. Stahl. In 1950 millions of gallons of frozen concentrate sold nationally under such names as Minute Maid, Snow Crop, and Donald Duck.

criticism elsewhere in the nation, however, about Florida's widespread use of Caribbean migrant workers in sugar-cane and vegetable fields where low pay, poor housing, and inadequate education and medical attention seemed to many a new form of labor exploitation that some called "sweatshops of the soil." The workers' plight would receive special attention in a much-praised CBS-TV documentary program of 1960 entitled "Harvest of Shame." Commercial ornamental horticulture was a new and thriving agribusiness. The bulk of Florida's manufacturing

By 1950 Florida's total cattle population ranked fourth in the Southeast and twenty-third in the nation. In beef cattle alone, where Florida had 550 registered herds and a total of one million animals on pastures and ranges, the state stood first in the Southeast and twelfth in the nation. The numbers resulted in part from a dipping program to eradicate the Texas fever tick that had ravaged Florida herds. Begun under legislative act in 1923, chemical dipping for tick was the innovation of an internationally celebrated Chicago socialite named Mrs. Potter (Bertha Honore) Palmer. In 1910, to the astonishment of her titled and posh friends, she had pulled up stakes and moved to the fishing village of Sarasota. There she bought 3,000 head of cattle, a wild, scrawny breed that dated from Spanish times. By running her cattle through dipping vats to rid them of ticks, and by importing Brahman bulls to produce a tick-free bloodline, the remarkable Bertha Palmer helped Florida produce the hardy, disease-resistant breeds found by midcentury.

industry continued to be closely tied to agriculture and forestry. Food-processing plants dominated the three thousand manufacturing establishments that could be counted in the state at midcentury: packinghouses, canneries, and frozen concentrate plants drew their raw material from citrus and vegetables. The number of cattle in the state made it fourth in the Southeast and twenty-third in the nation. If Florida had an industrial center as such, it was Tampa and Hillsborough County, where 16,000 workers were engaged in manufacturing of many different kinds, followed by Duval and Dade counties. Stores and shops flourished. Three-quarters of Floridians' $4 billion income was expended in retail purchases. In the years since the crash, total retail sales in the United States had increased by 170 percent, but in Florida the increase was 373 percent. Department stores such as Burdines, Cohen, and Maas prospered in the larger cities. Large chain supermarkets began to replace less efficient corner groceries.

In all, the business community was showing a new confidence, aggressiveness, and imagination. Florida's premier banker, flinty Ed Ball, of Jacksonville, presided over the Florida National Bank, with thirty institutions the largest chain in the state and the principal source of credit for business growth. Arguably the most powerful man in Florida, Ball also directed the enormous Alfred I. du Pont estate. Among other current and emerging business leaders in the state were members of the Howell Tyson Lykes family of Tampa, who were engaged in land, meat packing, citrus, and ocean transportation; Martin Andersen, publisher of the *Orlando Sentinel*; Ben Hill Griffin, Jr., Frostproof citrus grower and cattleman; bankers Alfred A. McKethan, of Brooksville, Alpheus L. Ellis, of Tarpon Springs, and Godfrey Smith, of Tallahassee; Jacksonville supermarket executive A. D. Davis; Charles Rosenberg, of Rose Printing Company, Tallahassee; McGregor Smith, board chairman of Florida Power and Light Company; publisher J.J. Daniel of Jacksonville; St. Petersburg merchant James Earl "Doc" Webb; and builders Jim Walter, of Tampa, and Marshall E. Rinker, of West Palm Beach.

In Brevard County a new complex of high technology industries was foreshadowed at Cape Canaveral on July 24, 1950, when a first rocket firing took place, a fifty-six-foot, two-stage WAC-Bumper missile incorporating a captured German V-2 and a U.S. Army–developed WAC Corporal rocket. Acquired the year before by the U.S. Air Force, the historic, triangular-shaped cape, with its 15,000 acres of brush, became the launching site for the nation's infant ballistic missile program. Its advantages included temperate, all-weather launching conditions, a geophysical benefit from the earth's rotation, and the proximity southeastward of tracking stations on the string of Caribbean islands. The first industries to be assigned responsibilities for operations, in 1953, were Pan American World Airways and the Radio Corporation of America. As the decade advanced, thousands of technicians and workers staffed these and a myriad of other space-oriented industries, and housing, schools, and other services multiplied rapidly in nearby Eau Gallie, Cocoa, Melbourne, and Titusville. Few if any observers of the space boom would be aware that this latitude of Florida had been predicted as the launching site of man's first voyage to the moon by French science fiction writer Jules Verne, in his book *From the Earth to the Moon*, published in Paris in 1865.

Because of the equalization formulas and new standards of the Minimum Foundation Program, Florida's half-million schoolchildren in K–12 studied under better teachers, with better textbooks, in improved classrooms where strict requirements, including 180-day school years, were enforced statewide. But problems posed by inadequate salaries and educational theory brought the public schools under widespread scrutiny by parents, teachers, school boards, and legislators during the fifties. Some of the central issues would still be under debate forty years later. Six junior colleges in existence by 1950, at St. Petersburg, West Palm Beach, Orlando, Jacksonville, Chipola, and Pensacola, presaged a solution to be adopted later in the fifties for Florida's burgeoning post–high school population. Eventually the state would have twenty-eight community colleges (as most came to be called) serving every region of the peninsula and Panhandle.

The Pepper-Smathers Campaign

Claude Pepper's bid for reelection to the U.S. Senate in 1950 attracted a massive campaign of political annihilation that was chiefly the work of "Mr. Ed." That Ed Ball threw his considerable clout against Florida's best-known politician did not surprise anyone who was aware that Ball and Pepper were not only political opposites but that they had long been engaged in a legal struggle for control of the Florida East Coast Railway (FEC), which was still in receivership. Ball found a new candidate in popular, civic club–handsome George A. Smathers, of Miami, who had been elected to the U.S. Congress in 1946 and 1948 with Pepper's help.

Smathers had pledged that he would never run against his mentor, but, courted by Ball and du Pont money, he changed his mind. Pepper was vulnerable principally because he was a leader of the liberal wing of the national Democratic party at a time when most of the country, including Florida, was swinging to the right and anti-Communist feeling was running high. Pepper's many New Deal positions were out of synchronization with the surging conservative mood in his home state.

Smathers, claiming that the senator had been taken in, if not subverted, by the Communists, labeled him "Red Pepper," a sobriquet that had considerable currency and effect. A forty-nine-page booklet attempted to link Pepper with various Communist front organizations. Pepper called it "the most scurrilous and vicious document to besmirch a Florida political campaign." Physicians, fearing "socialized medicine," enclosed anti-Pepper leaflets with their bills. In the end every major newspaper in the state but two, the *St. Petersburg Times* and the *Daytona Beach News Journal*, came out for Smathers. On primary election day 70 percent of the state's registered Democrats voted their choice in the highest turnout in Florida history. Smathers won by 67,000 votes, taking every east coast county on the FEC route except Dade, which he lost by only 917 votes.

Pepper had taken Dade by 10,000 votes just six years before. His resolute spirit led him to challenge Senator Spessard Holland for his seat in 1958, but he lost by 87,000 votes. Finally, in 1962, he won election to Washington as a member of the House of Representatives for the Third District in South Florida, and he won reelection thereafter until his death in 1989, becoming the principal legislative advocate for the elderly in the nation. George Smathers easily defeated his Republican opponent in the 1950 general election and served in the Senate from 1951 to 1969.

A reporter types his daily story on the campaign trail with Senator Claude Pepper in 1950. In a bitter struggle for reelection against George A. Smathers of Miami, whom he had once befriended, Pepper tried to fight off charges that he was soft on Communism and on socialized medicine. Smathers, heavily bankrolled by Ed Ball and du Pont money, distributed a carefully cropped photograph of Pepper posing at New York's Madison Square Garden with Paul Robeson, a black opera singer widely considered a Soviet sympathizer. The effect was damaging in a Florida that was very different in political outlook from the New Deal state of 1936 when Pepper had first been elected. His senate seniority and spellbinding oratory notwithstanding, Pepper lost.

The McCarty and Collins Years

By the end of Fuller Warren's administration in 1952 the Florida electorate was ready for a governor of professional capability, integrity, honesty, and common sense. The voters remembered that such a person had run second to Warren in the Democratic primary of 1948 and elected him:

Governor Dan McCarty in 1953 signs a $5 million appropriations bill for construction of the first building of what would become the J. Hillis Miller Health Center at the University of Florida. Standing to the left is the governor's brother and aide, John; at right is Earl P. Powers, chairman of the state Turnpike Authority. McCarty, a Fort Pierce citrus grower and cattleman, was the first governor from the southern part of the state. During his brief months-long term, ended by his untimely death, he established new standards based on merit and trust for appointments to administrative offices.

Daniel T. McCarty, of Fort Pierce, in 1941 the youngest person (age twenty-nine) ever elected Speaker of Florida's House of Representatives. Shortly after his inauguration as the first governor from the southern counties since Albert Gilchrist of Punta Gorda in 1909, McCarty suffered a disabling heart attack that kept him confined to bed for months. He continued to govern, using his aides to reorganize the road department; to create a turnpike commission to construct and operate the planned north-south toll highway; to centralize state purchasing; and to propose tax relief for those insurance companies that agreed to establish home or regional offices in Jacksonville. His weakened condition made him incapable finally of surviving a bad cold, which unexpectedly took his life on September 28, 1953. As the constitution provided, the president of the senate, Charley E. Johns of Starke, became governor. Subsequently, the state supreme court ruled that Johns would be *acting* governor and that a special election would be held in November 1954 to select a governor to complete McCarty's term.

Johns had served continuously since 1935 in the senate where the prominent insurance man (formerly a railroad conductor) had become a leader of the dominant rural northern wing of that body. From the outset of his administration, it was clear that he shared little of his immediate predecessor's political philosophy. Almost his first action was to refuse to sign thirty-one commissions for McCarty appointees and to suspend seventeen members of the "little cabinet." This return to the "spoils system" type of patronage with no regard for merit angered many Floridians who had looked to the McCarty governorship to correct similar dispensations under Warren. In October 1953, Johns announced his candidacy for a four-year term, and he faced formidable primary opposition in the person of LeRoy Collins, son of a Tallahassee grocer and longtime member of the legislature (1934–54), who was determined to reinstitute McCarty's platform. Collins won in 1954 and, because of his demonstrated integrity, progressive leadership, and personal magnetism, he won even more decisively (51.7 percent) against five Democratic opponents in the 1956 race for a full four-year term. With close to a three-to-one victory in the general election and strong progressive support from the lower east coast, Tampa Bay, and his home county of Leon, Collins embarked on an administration that historians rank as perhaps the most enlightened and successful in Florida's history. One of the founders of the "New South," he became the first governor actively to recruit business and industry to Florida. He initiated efforts to reapportion the legislature, where only 13.6 percent of the population, all in rural northern Florida, elected over one-half the members of the senate, and where the same

Ku Klux Klan members were a force for racism and bigotry in northern Florida from World War I into the 1960s. Many Floridians in the region rejected their presence and their white supremacy doctrine. Governor Fuller Warren, for one, called them "sheeted jerks." Klan members directed violence toward whites and blacks alike, flogging labor organizers in Tampa in the 1930s and inciting racists against black civil rights demonstrators in the 1960s. The burning cross rally shown here took place at Tallahassee on September 1, 1956.

counties controlled the senate presidency, the house speakership, and the majority committees in both houses. Underrepresented citizens had long come to say, "No man's life, family, or property is safe while the legislature is in session." Collins is best remembered for steering a moderate course in the integration crisis that erupted in the wake of the 1954 U.S. Supreme Court decision *Brown v. Topeka Board of Education.* Basically a conservative on the racial issue, he did not favor school integration, but he adopted a moderate stance that allowed integration to proceed, though

LeRoy Collins, governor from 1955 to 1961, represented Old South "hominy husker" values, such as church, hard work, fair play, and honesty, in combination with New South values of business pragmatism, social harmony, and governmental reform. In his first years as governor, which directly followed the U.S. Supreme Court decision of 1954 ending racial segregation in the nation's schools, Collins adopted the moderate stance of defending segregation while condemning defiance of the Court. Later in his administration he spoke of racial integration and civil rights as moral obligations, which enhanced his national stature but eroded much of his support in the state. In 1964–65 Collins served as director of the Community Relations Service in the administration of President Lyndon B. Johnson, in which capacity he won praise for his actions to prevent violence at a historic civil rights march in Selma, Alabama.

slowly, without the level of disorder found in other southern states.

In the end Collins's reapportionment efforts foundered on the rock of legislative intransigence, but what he began would succeed a decade later. Similarly, though he failed to modernize the 1885 constitution, another of his initiatives, that, too, would succeed a decade later. On reaching the end of his administration, one marked by business prosperity, stability of government, expansion of higher education, equity of the tax structure, and distinction for both himself and Florida (he served, for example, as chairman of both the National Governors' Conference and the Democratic National Convention), Collins moved on to various national appointive offices, both public and private. In 1968 he lost a bid in the general elections for a seat in the U.S. Senate. On his death in 1991, the state house of representatives unanimously named him "Floridian of the Century."

The decade from 1950 to 1960 produced a 78.7 percent growth rate in Florida's population, the highest in the state's history. (Growth rate in the 1980s would be 33.4 percent.) Immigrants from the Northeast tended to resettle on the Atlantic coast; those from the Midwest generally chose the Gulf and central counties. One reason for the vast influx of new residents was the availability of affordable room air conditioners that made inside-the-home living bearable for northerners unaccustomed to high heat and humidity. The advent of window units, however, caused the disappearance of the "front porch" society that Florida had long been, with the rocker, the swing, and the murmur of human voices.

The Sixties

No movement characterized Florida's political and social life in the 1960s as much as did civil rights for the state's long-neglected and much-abused African-American population. Even anti-Vietnam War and feminist sentiments that developed, principally among the young, toward the end of the decade failed to dislodge black rights as the overriding issue of the sixties. First to face significant black pressure was Governor Farris Bryant, a strong segregationist who took office in 1961. Municipal authorities had successfully resisted efforts by blacks to end segregated lunch counters, to end Jim Crow seating in public transportation, and to integrate city parks, golf courses, pools, and beaches. There had been racial disorders: demonstrations racked Jacksonville for several days, and a confrontation between whites and blacks in Tallahassee led to one black's death. In 1963–64 attention fastened on St. Augustine, where citizens were preparing for the four hundredth anniversary of the city in 1965. Though racial relations had been more benign in the "Ancient City" than in most other places, and its public schools were desegregated by 1964, quadricentennial visibility made it unusually vulnerable. Both white racists, mostly from outside, and antisegregation demonstrators, also mostly from outside, made the city's streets, pools, and beaches a dangerous battleground, drawing wide media coverage, particularly when Dr. Martin Luther King, Jr., assumed personal direction of the demonstrations. The unnecessarily explosive environment resulted from maladroit handling by both Governor Bryant and local authorities (as well as by certain religious leaders, clerical and lay). By the time federal judge Bryan Simpson issued injunctions and orders that brought the community under control, local residents noted with relief that no deaths or serious injuries had occurred. Whatever else may be said about the event, there is little doubt that the publicity generated by St. Augustine's travail provided impetus to passage of the nation's Civil Rights Act of 1964.

That act by itself was not enough to resolve Florida's long-term racial problems of poverty, cultural exclusion, discrimination in law enforcement, unequal schools, and narrow employment opportunities. In 1967, frustrated by the continued impact of these problems, blacks in seven Florida cities, north and south, took to the streets in angry demonstrations. Governor Haydon Burns, a former mayor of Jacksonville, responded with restraint, though, like Bryant before him, he provided no leadership to move Florida's citizens beyond racial peace to racial justice. Nor would his successor, the unpredictable and flamboyant Claude Kirk, Jr., first Republican chief executive to be elected in Florida since 1872.

Fishing became a major sport and recreation as well as a food source in Florida during the twentieth century. On weekends and after work Floridians fished the freshwater lakes and rivers for fighting black bass or for bream, catfish, or perch. Saltwater fishing off Florida's long shoreline attracted resident and tourist alike. Anglers used live bait or lures for a multitude of game fish that included the leaping, silver-scaled tarpon, bonefish, big pompano, and snook. Others walked the shallow bottoms of waterways at night with Coleman lanterns and gigged flounder or cast nets into the bays and surf for shrimp or mullet. The more adventurous (and well-to-do) anglers trolled from cabin cruisers in the Gulf Stream for sailfish and marlin, as described in Philip Wylie's "Crunch and Des" magazine stories. Here, Prime Beaudoin (left) and Donald Tully, of St. Augustine, display their tarpon catches in 1961.

When Fidel Castro assumed rule over Cuba in 1959, soon afterward establishing a Soviet Union–supported communist government, an estimated 500,000 Cubans fled that country during the next twenty years seeking freedom in the United States. Most settled in Dade County, bringing professional and business skills that transformed that region's economy and cultural life. Miami, whose downtown boomed while other U.S. inner cities declined, became an international metropolis and the leading center of Latin American banking. These thirteen refugees in a canvas boat were rescued by the U.S. Coast Guard in 1968 fifty miles east-southeast of Key West. Similar escapes, many very daring, continued into the 2000s.

A sit-in by young African-Americans at an F. W. Woolworth's lunch counter in March 1960 initiated the civil rights movement in Tallahassee. They were inspired by a similar action taken the month before by four black freshmen from North Carolina Agricultural and Technical College at a Woolworth's in Greensboro. Here blacks protest racial segregation at Tallahassee's motion picture theaters in 1963. The movement, which had also taken root at Jacksonville in 1960, spread to other cities in the northern counties, including St. Augustine, where Dr. Martin Luther King, Jr., led street demonstrations in 1964.

Kirk faced more than racial problems during his term, principally a Democratic legislature and cabinet with which he feuded regularly for four years, though it was alleged that he spent more time out of Tallahassee than at his desk. In an administration that was more showy than substantive he vetoed a nearly tenfold pay increase that the legislators had voted themselves, then dramatically signed each paycheck after the veto was overridden. He hired the private Wackenhut Corporation of Coral Gables to lead a statewide war on crime and defended successfully a $500-a-member "Governor's Club" that provided money for his travel. In 1968, his second year, he gained a Republican colleague when Edward Gurney was elected to the U.S. Senate, the first GOP senator from Florida since Reconstruction. For Democrats it was, or should have been, a foreshadowing of changes to come. In the same year Florida at last adopted a new constitution to replace the document of 1885. It provided for a lieutenant governor, a second elective term for the governor, an official cabinet, and other timely measures for state and local governments. Florida's teachers K-12 bolted their classrooms in an unprecedented strike but returned without the concessions they sought. In interracial affairs, Governor Kirk was visibly on the move throughout Florida, restoring order, exhorting, conciliating, and on occasion obstructing forced school busing, which he stoutly opposed: in Manatee County in 1970 he seized control of the schools to prevent their integration to a specific ratio by busing.

One major accomplishment of the sixties took several U.S. Supreme Court decisions (1962, 1964, 1967), and a district court order to bring about: reapportionment of the legislature. For decades the five most populous counties—Dade, Duval, Hillsborough, Pinellas, and Broward—had attempted to break the hammerlock of the rural northern counties, legislators from which were called the "Pork Chop Gang," a term invented by editorial writer James Clendinen of the *Tampa Tribune*. Now, at last, "one person, one vote" apportionment came to Florida, based on a plan worked out on his living room floor by Manning J. Dauer, chair of the Department of Political Science at the University of Florida. Dade County's representation jumped from one senator and three representatives to nine senators and twenty-two representatives.

The decade was capped by a Florida-originated journey of unparalleled human significance. On July 16, 1969, aboard a rocket flight called Apollo XI, three American astronauts lifted off from Cape Canaveral and, four days later, two of them walked on the surface of the moon. That most closely watched event in the history of humanity was followed by five more lunar landings through 1972.

The Seventies

Helped by wide electoral rejection of the razzle-dazzle, confrontation style of Claude Kirk, Democrats swept the

Claude R. Kirk, Jr., was the first member of the Republican party to be elected governor since 1872, defeating Democrat Robert King High of Miami, 821,190 votes to 668,233, with the help of conservative Democrats. The flamboyant Kirk, never out of the news, fought continually with the elected cabinet, all Democrats, and with the Democrat-controlled legislature. His administration, 1967–71, was the last in which a governor was limited to one four-year term. Permitted by the new constitution of 1969 to run again, he lost to Senator Reubin O'Donovan Askew, of Pensacola, who would serve out two terms.

statewide elections of 1970. Sedate, judicious Reubin Askew, a moderate liberal state senator from Pensacola, defeated the incumbent for governor, and another state senator, Lawton Chiles, won election to the U.S. Senate. During his eight years as governor—he was the first to be elected to

Six recent governors pose together in April 1973: C. Farris Bryant (1961–65), LeRoy Collins (1955–61), Charley E. Johns (1953–55), Reubin Askew (1971–79), Millard F. Caldwell (1945–49), and W. Haydon Burns (1965–67). In Florida's "weak governor–elected cabinet" system the governors have had limited executive authority. A governor sits on numerous administrative boards where his is just one vote among many—except the Pardon Board, where he has a limited veto. With no limitations on cabinet officers' terms and increasing division of the cabinet along party lines, Florida's "collegial executive" arrangement has not favored recent governors. In 1991 gubernatorial authority was trimmed still further when the Florida Supreme Court ruled that only the legislature could authorize cuts in the state budget.

two full terms—Askew took directly to the people numerous problems that the now-annual legislature could not resolve. By these progressive means he was able to secure statewide busing for schoolchildren, a Sunshine Law that required financial disclosure by all state officials, elected and appointed, and a state income tax on corporations.

The corporations tax, from which most corporations, then as now, were exempt, took account of the fact that mail order houses in Florida, where there was no corporate tax, were charging the same for goods as the identical corporations in Georgia, where there was such a tax. It also acknowledged an impressive flow of industry into the state in the previous two decades: Pratt and Whitney, Martin Aircraft, Sperry Rand, Maxwell House, IBM, Anheuser-Busch, and Disney World, which opened the Magic Kingdom in 1971 and Epcot Center in 1982 to become the world's largest paid attraction, drawing many more tourists each year than Florida had residents. This is not to slight Florida's native industries, such as phosphate, cattle, and frozen fruit juice concentrate, all of which boomed in the seventies, or to overlook other tourist attractions, new and old, that were expanding in the same period: Marineland, Sea World, Miami Seaquarium, Busch Gardens, Cypress Gardens, Kennedy Space Center, and Silver Springs, among others. A nostalgic observer might have regretted the fact that big-budget attractions were overwhelming the beaches, springs, gardens, gators, parrots, and orchids that were an earlier staple of tourism, but a realistic observer would think more of the vulnerability of an industry that could ill afford any diminution of automotive fuel, as happened in 1973–74 after the Arab oil embargo, or a national recession as happened beginning in 1990 when declines in tourist traffic not only affected the industry as such, but the resulting losses in sales tax revenues reduced funds available for educational, public safety, health, and human services.

Many of Florida's traditionally placid university students erupted in campus demonstrations against the Vietnam War in the early seventies. The University of Florida was scene of the most prominent disorders, provoked in 1970 by the student killings at Kent State and by the U.S. invasion of Cambodia, and in 1972 by the U.S. mining of Haiphong harbor in North Vietnam. Numerous student groups at Florida's universities had been active in anti-war, civil rights, environmental, and feminist movements since the mid-sixties, but social activism declined after the drawing down of the war and the coincidental Arab oil embargo and recession of 1973–74.

Askew failed in 1978 to change Florida's unique "weak governor–elected cabinet" form of administration, as he also failed to secure legislative approval of other reforms. When he left office in 1979, however, it was clear not only that his record had general public approval but that he had restored integrity and professionalism to the office of governor. His stature stood in stark contrast to that of three cabinet officers who were forced out of office and two supreme court justices who resigned under threat of impeachment, although he caught some dust from a legislative censure of his lieutenant governor, Tom Adams. At the same time, Republican U.S. Senator Gurney, indicted on bribery and conspiracy charges, decided not to run for reelection. In 1979, having served, like Collins, as chairman of the National Governors' Conference, and having given the keynote address at the Democratic National Convention, Reubin Askew joined President Jimmy Carter's administration as special trade representative, a cabinet-level post.

As the decade neared its end, a new $45 million skyscraper capitol opened its doors to a generally prosperous people, an optimistic legislature, and a newly inaugurated governor in the Askew mold: Dade County land developer and state senator Robert "Bob" Graham.

Within Our Memories

By 1980, for the first time, the total population of the American South and West exceeded that of the North and Midwest, and Florida with well over 9 million residents was the eighth largest state in the nation. Between 1930 and 1980 no other state had matched Florida's 564 percent rate of increase. Large federal grants had helped to sustain the growth. During the decade that followed, people poured across the state's borders from the Northeast and Midwest, as well as from the Caribbean and South America, in such numbers that 3 million additional residents raised Florida's standing by 1990 to fourth in the nation, behind Texas, New York, and California. As many as 950 to 1,000 new Floridians had been born in the state, Florida was now reckoned as a state "where everyone is from somewhere else."

The spiraling growth rate caused nine of Florida's cities to rank among the eleven fastest growing metropolitan areas in the country during the 1980s: Naples led all U.S. cities with a 77 percent increase, followed by Fort Pierce with 66 percent; other Florida cities in the top eleven were Fort Myers, Ocala, Orlando, West Palm Beach, Melbourne-Titusville, Daytona Beach, and Bradenton. North Florida, which a century before accounted for over 70 percent of the population, shared comparatively little in the boom. By 1990 less than 17 percent of the population was rural, and 85 percent of the state's population lived within ten miles of either coast, although intense housing development, much of it for retirees, was appearing in the south-central counties. Retirees, in fact, accounted for almost 50 percent of the population growth in the decade. Taking in good humor the description of its retirement havens as "God's Waiting Room," Florida valued its senior arrivals who brought with them good citizenship standing and steady incomes from Social Security and pensions. Charlotte County on the lower Gulf Coast, where residents over sixty years of age accounted for only 10.8 percent of the population in 1950, had the highest median age (56.8 years) of all Florida's counties forty years later. The lowest median age, 26.5, belonged to Alachua County with its large university population.

The state's various ethnic concentrations were evidence of another distinct source of immigration. Thirty different ethnic groups, apart from U.S. Anglo-Americans and African-Americans, had a role in creating modern Florida. They included, among those of European origin, Minorcans, Italians, Spaniards, Germans, Greeks, Irish, Danes, Swedes, Poles, Dutch, Slovaks, and French-Canadians. A large colony of American Jews, most from New York City, came in the 1930s and 1940s to Miami and Miami Beach, first as tourists and later as year-round residents (including after 1960 many retirees). They doubled their numbers every five years until the 1980s, when, owing mainly to dispersal to neighboring counties, the city and beach figures began a marked decline. A notable concentration of immigrants in the Miami metropolitan area has been the

Resident Louis Maltz reads the Torah at Biscayne Bay, Miami, in 1973. The first Florida Jews settled in Pensacola as early as the 1760s. Early synagogues were Temple Beth-El, established at Pensacola in 1874, and Temple Ahavath Chesed at Jacksonville in 1882. A survey conducted in 1881 showed 772 Jews in Florida, of whom 130 lived in Jacksonville. In 1913 seventy-five Jewish residents in Miami founded congregation B'nai Zion, later renamed Beth David. A large colony of Jews, most from New York City, settled in Miami and Miami Beach beginning in the 1930s. Their population doubled every five years until the 1980s, when many moved to neighboring counties. Today 600,000 Jews live in Dade, Broward, and Palm Beach counties, the highest concentration outside New York City and Los Angeles. Another 150,000 live elsewhere in the state.

Cuban exile community. Thousands of Cuba's most accomplished middle- and upper-class families fled Fidel Castro's revolutionary society in the years 1959–62 and built new lives, mostly prosperous and militantly anticommunist, in Miami. Additional exiles came in 1965–73 and lent momentum to the "Hispanization" of large areas of the city, particularly the "Little Havana" section of downtown.

A third migration, the so-called Mariel boat lift of 1980, brought 123,000 more Cubans to U.S. shores, but since U.S. authorities determined that some had criminal records, not all were permitted to join the Miami community. By 1980, Cubans numbered 60 percent of the city's population; percentages in outlying communities sometimes ran higher. During the 1980s, swelled by additional immigration from El Salvador, Nicaragua, Colombia, Venezuela, and the Dominican Republic, Miami would become a major center of Latin American banking, trade, and culture. Where the rich new Latin contributions to Florida life might lead historians to speak of the Second Spanish Conquest, social scientists, focusing on the generally separatist character of Cuban culture, might find themselves reminded that Florida was less a melting pot than it was a mixed salad. By 1990 Haitians were displacing Canadians as the second largest immigrant category.

For most of Florida's history as a part of the United States, African-Americans formed nearly one-half of the population. The numbers fell below 30 percent by 1930, owing to black migration north (after 1915) in search of industrial employment. At that date 44 percent lived in urban areas. By the 1980s the urban percentage had risen to 85 percent, highest in the South. An increase in the number of black elected and appointed city officials meant an increase in the number of blacks in the police forces (which led to a decline in police brutality) and in sleep-over fire departments. It also led to an increase of paved streets in black neighborhoods. In face of the huge white and Hispanic immigration in recent decades, however, blacks lost further position by 1990 when they made up only 14.5 percent of Florida's residents, and, though many owned their home and ran their own businesses, they experienced declining political influence as a result. The problem of lessened political participation was not helped by the fact that, though Florida was led in the 1970s and through much of the 1980s by progressive governors (Askew and Graham), its political culture remained decidedly conservative.

The same fragmentation of Florida's political culture that V.O. Key, Jr., found in 1949 continued apace in the 1980s. If Greater Miami could be described as a collection of municipalities in search of a city, Florida was a collection of cities in search of a state. The circulation zones of eleven major newspapers defined eleven divergent provinces; no visible glue other than a statewide television broadcast bound them together. Add to that Balkanization the divisions that arose from out-of-state birthplace loyalties, ethnic and race distinctions, political localism, marked age differences, physical distances, internal rootlessness (one child out of five changed school each year), and the growing separation of the affluent who lived in enclaves behind guard gates from the majority poor whose numbers were expanding—with a shrinking middle class in between—and one had a state with no discernible coherence or unity.

Seeking to make demographic sense out of fractured Florida in 1990, the *Miami Herald* thought it found four distinct political regions in: (1) the Panhandle west of Jacksonville, including the north-central counties, (2) the Miami-Fort Lauderdale-Palm Beach megalopolis, (3) the lower Gulf Coast, and (4) the I-4 corridor, or midsection, from Daytona Beach to Orlando and Tampa-St. Petersburg. Certain exceptions stood out from this template, such as Tallahassee and Gainesville, but the model was probably as good as the beginning of the 1990s could provide. Of interest to political scientists was the finding that between 1980 and 1990 the number of Democrats among Florida voters remained fairly stable, while the percentage of Republicans increased toward a position of parity.

Women dramatically improved their position in Florida's political leadership. Whereas in 1950 no women held congressional, statewide, or mayoral offices, and there was only one woman in the legislature, in 1990 there were one woman in Congress, one in the state cabinet, ten in the state senate, twenty in the house, and fifty-five in mayoral offices. Similar advances could be found in county commissions and school boards around the state.

Although there were signs by 1988 that state growth was slowing, there was no indication that the myriad problems that growth had created were similarly subsiding. Florida's infrastructure was stretched to the breaking point: Florida required *each day* one mile of new highway, two new K-12 classrooms, as many new teachers, two more police officers, three more state prison beds, and 178 more gallons of water per person. With a limited tax base and no income tax, Florida was progressively unable to meet its staggering needs. Residents of the lower Gulf Coast pressed for a new university to serve that region; meanwhile, with a forty-ninth ranking among the states in per capita support of higher education, Florida was barely funding the state universities that already existed. Business and housing development, furthermore, had been almost without plan or design, with the result that in many places Florida's once pristine landscapes were marred by uncontrolled urban sprawl with its ugly strip malls, garish signs, crackerbox architecture, overstretched utilities, and congested streets. A trip down International Drive, U.S. Highways 192 and 17–92, South Orange Blossom Trail, and State Road 436 in the central counties conveyed enough shock value to persuade even the most buoyant Floridians that some parts of their state were descending into terminal tackiness. The Growth Management Act passed in the decade was expected by state and local leaders to correct some of that disorder.

To human-generated problems one must add the occasional "act of God," such as the billion-dollar "Christmas freeze" of 1983 that destroyed citrus groves above Orlando; the two-day freeze in January 1985 that hit as far south as Palm Beach-Naples, killing 20 percent of the orange and grapefruit crop, two-thirds of the winter vegetables, and a third of Florida's grazing land; and the equally destructive freeze of Christmas Eve 1989. As a result of these low-temperature events, citrus production moved farther south on the peninsula. By 1992 the leading citrus counties, in order, were St. Lucie, Hendry, and Indian River. Citrus and Orange counties became misnomers. Reminding Florida that its

Edward Ball, who managed the giant du Pont estate, is shown with his sister, Mrs. Alfred I. (Jessie) du Pont. From the 1930s to his death in 1981, Ball exercised unprecedented political influence over the northern rural delegations in the legislature, and his economic leverage throughout Florida was matched by no other individual. Yet the five-foot-six financier lived frugally in a Jacksonville hotel apartment, operated out of an austere office, wore dime store glasses, and listed his occupation as "farmer." Each day at quitting time he gathered his associates and lifted a glass of bourbon with the toast "Confusion to the enemy."

vulnerabilities were not all of the cold weather sort, Hurricane Andrew hit south Dade County on August 24, 1992, leaving 41 people dead and more than 200,000 homeless. Andrew did approximately $15.5 billion in property damage and was the costliest natural disaster in American history. On February 23, 1998, a swarm of tornadoes, the deadliest ever recorded in the state, ripped through central Florida and claimed 42 lives.

Increasingly worrisome to many Floridians was the risk that the state's growth presented to fragile ecosystems. A vigorous lay environmental movement pushed legislators to protect Florida's shallow aquifer from water contamination; to preserve the wetlands that kept the peninsula, one of the few such green landmasses at this latitude, from being a desert; to save the dying Everglades and to correct the improvident channeling of rivers such as the Kissimmee; to control the chemical runoff of fertilizers and pesticides into water resources; to acquire environmentally sensitive lands such as swamps, marshes, and beaches; to provide effective control over flooding, drainage, sewage, and hazardous waste disposal; and to protect Florida's unique endangered animal species such as roseate spoonbill, panther, sea turtle, and manatee. One pronounced success of the environmental movement was the halting of the Cross-Florida Barge Canal, begun in 1964 and stopped in 1971, which would have destroyed numerous important natural land features, including the Ocklawaha wilderness river and valley. Eventually, the northern counties through which the ill-advised canal would have passed received back the affected lands for use as nature preserves and recreation areas.

Even more troubling to Floridians during the 1980s was the state's crime rate, highest in the nation. The state's prison population at decade's end was the nation's fourth largest, its death row population the second largest. A disproportionately high number of all inmates were high school dropouts. Because of prison overcrowding, inmates on time served only 37 percent of their sentences before returning to the streets. Over half of Florida's residents, according to a 1989 poll, were afraid to walk outside their homes in the evening. Drug abuse and the drug trade were the most visible crime areas, leading to billions of dollars spent on marijuana and cocaine interdiction, police work, court costs, medical costs, and insurance rates. In Miami, for most of the decade a leading center of the nation's drug importation and money "laundering" problems, Colombian drug smugglers called "cocaine cowboys" engaged in shootouts on the streets. But the illicit drug dealerships, portrayed in a popular television program, "Miami Vice," were also at work as far away as the Gulf counties in North Florida, where private aircraft and fast motorboats made

With the exception of the fantasy towers and futuristic globe at Disney's Magic Kingdom and Epcot Center, near Orlando, probably no architectural image has been more identified with Florida than the white, sunsplashed hotel row of Miami Beach. Since the 1980s, the municipality has enjoyed a resurgence of tourism and night life. Hotels, restaurants, and watering holes, particularly on trendy South Beach, are filled with tourists and local revelers. A new beach and boardwalk have been constructed since this photo. A younger crowd than the beach has seen in years is restoring some of the glitter and glamour that the resort had in 1964–70, when "The Jackie Gleason Show" originated "from the sun and fun capital of the world." Nearby hotel row is an Art Deco district with the largest concentration of that architectural style in the country—the only style that made a conscious break with the past and looked forward to the future.

drug drops to cohorts, who sold the current drug of choice, now "crack" cocaine, to a constituency that included Florida's young. The most thoughtful state's leaders were concerned that more had to be done to meet crime problems from the nursery up rather than from death row down. Civic and religious spokespersons began talking in earnest about the need to protect, nurture, and guide

Florida's young, all the more so when it became known that the state had the nation's highest youth suicide rate.

During his eight-year administration, Governor Graham launched several funded programs to preserve Florida's natural and scenic environment. They carried names such as Save Our Rivers, Save Our Coasts, and Save Our Everglades. He also focused Floridians' attention on the need for quality improvement in education, if the state was to attract business and industry from other regions of the country. During his two terms, one million new jobs were created, including 93,000 in manufacturing. Health care, especially for the elderly, also occupied the attention of the governor's staff. Graham faced several acute socioeconomic problems, among them a truckers' strike in 1979 that nearly paralyzed commerce and forced him to call out the National Guard; the unexpected immigration into South Florida in 1980 of 160,000 Cuban and Haitian refugees for whom the state, with few resources, had to provide space and support; in Dade County a black Liberty City riot in the same year, leading to eighteen deaths, white and black, that revealed long pent-up frustrations over inadequate housing, economic opportunities, schools, transit, and recreational facilities as well as the immediately precipitating cause of the event, alleged police brutality; and throughout the eighties the drug trade—some thought it close to being Florida's largest industry—that led to an increase of 102 percent in cocaine-related arrests during the decade. In 1987 Graham stepped down three days before the end of his term (permitting Lieutenant Governor Wayne Mixson to serve as governor for that period) in order to take the oath of office as U.S. senator, the third former governor to do so.

In 1986 former mayor of Tampa Robert "Bob" Martinez became the second elected governor from his party since Reconstruction, and Republicans also scored gains in Congress, the legislature, and the state cabinet. Martinez got off to an uncertain start when he first supported, then disavowed, a tax on services that would have enlarged the state's tax base, and his appointments signaled to some a return to the "spoils system" of Governors Cone, Sholtz, Johns, Bryant, Burns, and Kirk. His bid for a second term failed.

Florida's "river of grass," the Everglades, is a vast sheet of fresh water that nourishes the entire penin-sula south of Lake Okeechobee. In recent years it has struggled to survive the polluting influence of mercury and nutrients such as phosphates and nitrates, most of them runoff from the sugar planta-tions, winter vegetable fields, and dairy farms that border the storied waters and their once abundant wildlife. As the 1990s began, environmentalists were encouraged by new state and federal initiatives taken to save the Glades, including purchase of 108,000 acres to enlarge the Everglades National Park—the largest environmental purchase since the creation of Big Cypress Preserve in 1974. A new state-federal strategy to purify the Everglades water and save endangered species became law in De-cember 2000. An increasing number of Floridians seem convinced that how well they manage their aquifers, wetlands, and other precious water resources will determine Florida's future standard of living for them and all other living creatures.

Former U.S. senator Lawton Chiles won election to the office of governor in November 1990. From a law practice in Lakeland, he had advanced to the state legislature for twelve years and to the U.S. Senate for eighteen. A Democrat in a state that was turning Republican in leadership, the genial, folksy Chiles pursued a moderate course in policy initiatives and, to the amazement of some, won re-election in 1994 in a close vote over a popular young Republican challenger, Jeb Bush of Miami, son of former president George H. W. Bush. As he began his second term, he was the only Democrat presiding over a heavily populated state.

Chiles's nearly eight years in the governor's mansion are remembered for his advocacy of health programs for children, one of which led to a 26 percent decline in infant mortality; for campaign finance reform; and for leadership in securing a $13.2 billion settlement from the tobacco industry for the health care costs incurred by Florida citizens who used tobacco products. Twenty-three days shy of completing his second term, Chiles died at home from a sudden heart abnormality. He was succeeded for the remainder of his term by Lieutenant Governor Kenneth "Buddy" MacKay, the first to succeed to the office of governor of Florida upon the death of his predecessor since Marcellus Lovejoy Stearns filled the office of Governor Ossian Hart, who died of pneumonia in 1874.

Florida's two U.S. senators are Democrats. In 2000 nearly 19 percent of the state's 9.2 million registered electorate were independents or third-party voters. But the growing strength of the Republican party in Florida was evident in the elections of 1996, when, after more than a century of trying, it gained a majority in the state house of representatives. Two years later, it controlled the state senate as well. Florida had not suddenly been invaded by GOP stalwarts; their numbers had been increasing incrementally for years. Many conservative Democrats who had long been Republicans in all but name had either changed parties or crossed over in general elections. The Democrats still held the edge in the number of party members registered to vote, but the Republicans had done a better job of getting their voters to the polls. And in 1998 that held true in the race for governor.

In 1944 the Miami Herald had written, "It will be a cold day in hell when anyone from Miami is elected governor of Florida." It snowed in Tallahassee when Bob Graham of Miami Lakes was first inaugurated governor in 1979. And on January 6, 1999, the temperature was 30 degrees with a wind chill of 14 when Republican Jeb Bush of Miami, having vanquished Buddy MacKay in the gubernatorial election, took the oath of office as the state's forty-third governor. In a ten-minute inaugural address he envisioned a more limited role for government: "I want to protect people, not bureaucracies," he stated, and, continuing a theme of Lawton Chiles, promised to protect "the frailest and weakest among us." Bush was reelected in November 2002. It is too early for the historian to attempt an assessment of his accomplishments in office.

Changing Times

As Florida entered the twenty-first century, its people became aware of major shifts in population, increased threats to ecosystems, tremors in the job market, deficiencies in public education, and voting irregularities. The 2000 census confirmed what had long been suspected, namely, that the state's population growth rate was in decline. During the previous decade the number of permanent residents had increased by 23.5 percent to 15,982,378, entitling Florida to two additional members in the U.S. House of Representatives and two additional votes in the Electoral College. But the growth rate had been 33 percent in the 1980s and 44 percent in the 1970s. In 1990 eight of the ten fastest-growing metropolitan areas in the nation were in Florida; in 2000 only Naples made that list. Interestingly, Georgia's growth rate in the 1990s, 26.4 percent, made it the fastest-growing state in the South.

Environmentalists were consoled by the numbers, since they meant relief to vanishing greenspace and freshwater supplies. But demographers pointed to the fact that most of the growth came in the form of young people and young families, immigrants mainly from the Northeast and Midwest, who were having children at a higher rate than that at which the elderly population was dying. That placed new pressure on the state's already overstretched K-12 public school systems. Moreover, many retired and elderly people, who had already educated their own children, were disinclined to pay taxes for the education of younger people's children. Demographer Harold Hodgkinson has written, "Florida educators need to become skilled at convincing the elderly that their security in old age will be paid for by the wages of today's school children when they become workers. . . . Support of schools must be seen as a civic responsibility, not just a parental one."

Florida's African-American citizenry showed no growth during the decade, registering 14.6 percent of the population. Meanwhile, the Hispanic/Latino population (fueled by the immigration of 1 million people from Nicaragua, El Salvador, Mexico, Colombia, the Dominican Republic and other Latin countries) reached 2.7 million people, or 16.8 percent of the whole, surpassing the number of blacks in the state for the first time. While the general public tends to identify the Hispanic/Latino population with Miami, where the well-established and politically powerful Cuban-Americans are highly visible, it is a fact that other Hispanics/Latinos have outnumbered Cubans since 1990. Many of the new arrivals have dispersed into Florida's rural areas—for example, to Wauchula, Bowling Green, and Zolfo Springs in Hardee County, where Mexicans make up about one-quarter of the population. Some 5,000 Maya Indians, exiles from the civil war in Guatemala, work in the fields of Indiantown, Immokalee, and Homestead. A thriving community of 1,000 Salvadorans has found work in the nurseries, tomato-packing plants, and lumber industries of Quincy, west of Tallahassee.

Florida has always been a haven for immigrants—and not just for those who came from the northeastern states to settle in the Atlantic coast counties or from the midwestern states to make their homes on the Gulf of Mexico, nor just for those others who came from the Caribbean and from "south of the border." Spaniards from Iberia were the first immigrant group to arrive here. African-Americans, who were forced to come here, were the second. Everywhere in Florida today, one sees families of many national origins: Anglo-Saxons and Celts in the northern counties; Greeks in Tarpon Springs; Italians in Key West and Tampa; Haitians in Palm Beach and Broward Counties; Finns in Lake Worth; Danes in White City; Poles in Korona; African Bahamians in Miami; Syrian-Lebanese in Jacksonville; Asians in Miami, Tampa, St. Petersburg, Orlando, and Jacksonville; Minorcans in St. Augustine; and Canadians everywhere.

Indeed, by the year 2000 it was clear that Florida was a multicultural state with few parallels elsewhere. Contemporary efforts to "build community" have to engage with a great many faces from around the globe—faces that express a wide variety of racial and cultural attributes; faces that are retirement-village-old and kindergarten-young. Can unum be created out of such pluribus? The nation has answered yes. No doubt Florida will answer the same.

The 1990s exhibited another striking feature of today's Florida experience: in-migration, that is, movement of individuals and families from place to place within Florida. We have already noted the departure of most of the large Jewish population from Miami and Miami Beach to Broward and Palm Beach Counties. Close on their heels has been the flight of tens of thousands of non-Hispanic whites and upwardly mobile Hispanics and blacks, also to Broward, and beyond. What was happening in Miami-Dade County (changed from "Dade" in November 1997) that caused this diaspora? Among the answers given by observers are: drug murders, home invasions, and corruption of public officials on a scale that rivaled Boss Tweed's New York City in the 1860s and '70s; wasted public money (read: Metrorail system); choking traffic gridlocks that caused the former "Magic City" to become the nation's third most congested city; general poverty, making Miami the fourth poorest major city in the country; sardine-can classrooms; the final paving over of paradise; and the decision of many who lost their homes in 1992's Hurricane Andrew to take their insurance money and move northward. Not only families have fled, but also businesses and corporations, including Knight Ridder, the nation's second largest newspaper chain, Blockbuster, and all major bank headquarters.

The effect of this in-migration on Broward County has been dramatic. In 1997 the population density of Miami-Dade was about 982 persons per square mile; smaller Broward had 1,180 persons per square mile. Demographers expect that many in the moving mass will leave Broward behind for Palm Beach, St. Lucie, and Brevard Counties. Already, advance elements of the diaspora have discovered the woodlands and grassy meadows of north central Florida. One may even conjecture that the multitudes, having finally reached the Georgia border, will collide with the hordes fleeing south from Atlanta. Florida writer Carl Hiaasen has commented that people move to Florida "in pursuit of a dream that's being obliterated by their own footprints. It's a dream they're destined to chase from one end of the state to the other, trying to escape all the other dreamers."

When naturalist William Bartram toured east and west Florida in 1774 (see page 20), he recorded a vivid word portrait of the unspoiled "Elysian fields and green plains" he traversed, with their abundant flora and fauna. Here was the "glorious apartment," as he called it, of primeval Florida, before the arrival of concrete, asphalt, and contaminants. By 2000, of course, much of the natural beauty and freshness of old Florida was gone. Many once-pristine plains, waterways, and atmospheres have been built-over, paved, canalized, drained, dammed, fogged, or envenomed by pollutants. However, within the last six decades an aroused citizenry has been fighting back against that tide, to save what is left of the Florida that led them to move here or, if born here, to stay.

Early conservationist leaders included women's club activist May Mann Jennings and landscape architect Ernest F. Coe, who were instrumental in founding the Everglades National Park; Marjory Stoneman Douglas, whose eloquent book *The Everglades: River of Grass* (1947) became the landmark rationale for Everglades restoration; Nathaniel Reed of Hobe Sound, who, as U.S. assistant secretary of the

interior (1971–77), led the movement to save Lake Okeechobee; Marjorie Harris Carr of Gainesville, who almost
single-handedly stopped the Cross-Florida Barge Canal,
which would have introduced salt water into the Floridan
Aquifer; and Governor Claude Kirk, who forced a halt to
construction of a jetport in the Everglades, led the effort to
establish Biscayne National Park, and signed pioneer
water-quality and wetlands-protection acts into law.

In increasing numbers, cities and counties have turned to
the task of cleaning up Florida's lakes and rivers. Many
once-clear bodies of water have been defiled by industry,
overdevelopment, and careless dumping. The Florida Department of Environmental Protection (DEP) reported in
1998 that only about 50 percent of the state's lakes and waterways were clean enough for recreation and fishing.
However, industrial discharge into waterways had been
greatly curtailed, the DEP stated, and the principal remaining problem was development: rain falling onto
streets and lawns in developed areas causes runoff of oil,
fertilizers, pesticides, and similar pollutants into nearby
waterways. In 2000 a state task force issued a somber report
on Florida's storied freshwater springs. Some 600 in
number, more than in any other state, the springs are a dis-
tinctive feature of the central and northern counties, where
they form openings through limestone layers to the
Floridan Aquifer beneath. At this date, many of those
springs are covered in part by ugly green algae or exotic
plant growth such as hydrilla; many are fouled by sewage
and stormwater from nearby cities or by nitrates (the pollutants associated with fertilizers, animal manure, and septic
tanks); and still others are drying up because too much
groundwater is being pumped out for cities, farms, and
golf courses.

Most emblematic of the environmentalists' concerns has
been the dying Everglades. That lush, roadless wilderness,
three-fourths the size of West Virginia, is a unique mosaic
of water, sawgrass, mangrove shorelines, and hardwood
hammocks. Barely hanging on to survival amidst this
unique habitat are 68 threatened or endangered species of
mammals, birds, amphibians, and reptiles. The villainous
intruder has been chemical runoff of fertilizers and pesti-

cides from sugar plantations, winter vegetable fields, and dairy farms that border the sheets of water coursing south from Okeechobee to Florida Bay. Damage of a different kind has come from direct human intervention. In a misguided project to drain the glades for farmland and housing, the Army Corps of Engineers created a 1,000-mile network of canals, levees, and pumping stations that over the last half-century has had the unfortunate effect of obliterating about 50 percent of the historic wetlands and of squandering out to sea fresh drinking water sorely needed by South Florida's teeming populations.

Salvation for the "River of Grass" finally came in November-December 2000, when Congress passed and President Bill Clinton signed a $7.8 billion measure to clean and restore the natural flow of glades water. The Comprehensive Everglades Restoration Act, which had overwhelming bipartisan support, calls for a massive 38-year-long project to reverse the damage done. By any measure it will be the largest ecological rescue ever attempted. And the State of Florida will pick up half the tab.

In 1999 Florida's gross state product of $60,000 per worker was about 10 percent below the average in other southeastern states and about 20 percent below the national average. While job creation during the decade surpassed the rate of population increase, most openings have been in low-income positions in or connected to the tourism and hospitality industries. Florida's is primarily a service economy based on attractions, hotels and motels, car rentals, restaurants, fast food, and gas. There is a strong need for clerks, groundskeepers, janitors and maids, waiters and waitresses. In the metro Orlando area, where there is essentially full employment, most of it is in minimum-wage, low-skills, high turnover jobs, the per capita income is $3,000 less than the national average, and one out of eight employees works more than one job. Florida's current strength in technology—in 2000 the state placed sixth among the 50 states in the number of high-tech jobs (194,000) in, for example, semiconductors, lasers, and optics—provides better opportunities for the available skilled labor force. The technology industries are centered around research universities and along the so-called Silicon Beach stretching between Cape Canaveral and Miami.

The primary economic question facing Florida in the new global economy is whether it will have the educated work force to create and to attract additional high-tech industries, and to provide a high-skills, better-paid labor supply. The state's present low standing and recent declines in educational achievements have set alarm bells ringing. At the university level in 1999, the production of 15.9 science and engineering doctoral degrees per 100,000 working-age population gave Florida a rank of 40th in the nation. In baccalaureate degrees, Florida's eleven public colleges and universities rank 44th among the states. In funding per student they rank 45th. Where in 1990–91 Florida ranked 21st in state expenditures per pupil in the K-12 years, by 2000–2001 that ranking had fallen to 42nd; among the southeastern states only Alabama (43rd) and Tennessee (45th) rank lower. In high school graduation rates the state ranks 45th. Only two out of ten students who enter high school will complete a baccalaureate degree.

A 2002 study (New Cornerstone) funded by the Florida Chamber of Commerce concludes that "The cumulative impact of these and other breakdowns in Florida's education and workforce development systems is enormous." It points out that educational deficiencies weaken a state's economy by limiting the available number of high-skills workers; those talented graduates who find no openings in technology jobs move out of state; and increasing numbers of high school students, similarly seeing no challenging jobs, forego higher education, thus completing what the Chamber study calls "a vicious cycle."

A close election for U.S. president in 1876, when Rutherford B. Hayes won Florida's four electoral votes by fewer than 100 ballots, was mentioned on page 50. A similarly razor-thin but immensely more complicated vote for president took place here 124 years later, between Republican George W. Bush, brother of Florida's governor, and Democrat Al Gore. Too close to call on election day, November 7, 2000, the returns were contested for 36 chaotic days. Among the many points at issue between the two parties were confusing ballots (the "butterfly" ballot used in Palm

Beach County was a particular object of complaint); defective punchcard voting machines that, it was argued, did not perforate ballots cleanly but left "hanging," "pregnant," or "dimpled" chads; undervotes and overvotes; the right or obligation of counties to conduct recounts; manual recounts versus machine recounts; complaints from blacks and others that they were denied their right to vote by faulty purges of voting rolls or broken machines; and the deadline date by which Secretary of State Katherine Harris should officially certify the election results. The arguments moved through state circuit courts, U.S. district courts, a federal appeals court, the state supreme court, and the U.S. Supreme Court. In the end, Secretary Harris certified that Bush had won Florida and its 25 electoral votes by a margin of 537 votes. And on December 12, by a 5-to-4 vote, the U.S. Supreme Court ratified that decision. Although Gore had won the national popular vote, Bush had won the electoral college vote and the presidency.

This short review of the titanic struggle only touches on its complexities. A plethora of books and articles delve into the details. Some are partisan; some attempt to be objective. To date the most comprehensive review of the balloting, published on November 12, 2001, was conducted by a national consortium of eight news organizations, assisted by professional statisticians. It found that if, as Gore demanded, hand recounts of rejected ballots had been allowed to proceed in four predominantly Democratic counties—Miami-Dade, Broward, Palm Beach, and Volusia—Bush still would have won Florida by a small margin. On the other hand, it also concluded that if the courts had ordered a hand recount of rejected ballots in all 67 counties, Gore "might have won." Certainly the study of Florida's role in the most wrenching and disputed presidential election in American history will continue for many years to come.

The single point on which all studies so far have agreed is that Florida's election system failed the voters. Registration and balloting procedures stood in need of fundamental repair. To that end, in 2001 the state legislature passed the Florida Election Reform Act, which eliminated punchcard machines, provided for a uniform statewide ballot design, provided $32 million to the counties for new equipment, and established standards for manual recounts.

The Past Is Prologue

Wherever one travels today in the State of Florida, there are visible reminders of the ancient times that became statehood times, that became modern times, that became, at last, our times: shell middens and burial mounds, arrowheads and pottery left in fields where ghostly campfires seem still to burn; Spanish shell-rock castle walls at St. Augustine and the cannon of four nations at Fort Pickens on Pensacola Beach; land features that retain the names conferred on them by the indigenous tribes or by European captains who first navigated the coasts and explored the forested interior; underground foundations of Franciscan mission churches, now being excavated by archaeologists; dark rivers slumbering under oak canopies where, first, Indian canoe, then paddlewheel steamboat once coursed; towns and villages erected by American pioneers from thirty different national or ethnic stocks; farmlands cleared and cultivated by African-Americans, first as slaves, then as freedmen, eventually as Americans demanding to be Americans; railroads and automobile roads cut out of the pine flatlands or laid across the swamps and prairies; miles of citrus groves ranging as distant as the eye can see; industrial plants to process timber or phosphate, to manufacture computer chips or durable goods; and today's broad superhighways that wind past horse farms, retirement communities, international airports, launch pads, futuristic attractions, and come to rest, finally, amidst the gleaming towers of Oz-like cities.

One hundred and forty-five years ago, George R. Fairbanks, the first historian of Florida in the English language, in remarks made before the founding members of the Florida Historical Society, took note of that centuries-long procession of people and events in Florida up to the year in which he spoke: "Everything [around us] recalls the past," he said, and "provokes an earnest desire to look into that past, to draw out its secrets, and to bring back to our own minds and memories the scenes and actions of the olden time; and when our day shall in its turn be numbered with the past, and others shall have succeeded us, as we now fill the places of the generations who on this spot have been born and died, it may well be that a tribute of affectionate respect and reverence may be then bestowed upon us." So might we say today— and hope we are deserving.

Books on Florida History

The following select list of fifty-five Florida history titles will introduce the general reader to the wide array of books about Florida's past. Not all of these titles are still in print, though a surprisingly large number can be purchased through bookstores; but all are available in libraries and through interlibrary loan. Much of the literature about Florida history has appeared not in book form but in articles, as, for example, those in the *Florida Historical Quarterly*. Current and back issues of the *Quarterly* are available in most libraries. The reader should also inquire locally about regional historical journals and newsletters, such as *Tequesta: The Journal of the Historical Association of Southern Florida*; *Tampa Bay History*; *Gulf Coast Historical Review*; and *El Escribano: The St. Augustine Journal of History*.

General Histories

Abbey, Kathryn Trimmer (Kathryn Hanna). *Florida, Land of Change*. Chapel Hill: University of North Carolina Press, 1941.

Colburn, David R., and Jane L. Landers, eds. *The African-American Heritage of Florida*. Gainesville: University Press of Florida, 1995.

Derr, Mark. *Some Kind of Paradise: A Chronicle of Man and the Land in Florida*. Reprint. Gainesville: University Press of Florida, 1997.

Douglas, Marjory Stoneman. *The Everglades: River of Grass*. 1947. Rev. ed. Miami: Banyan Books, 1978.

Gannon, Michael, ed. *The New History of Florida*. Gainesville: University Press of Florida, 1996.

Hoffman, Paul E. *Florida's Frontiers*. Bloomington: Indiana University Press, 2002.

Tebeau, Charlton. *A History of Florida*. 1971. Rev. ed. Coral Gables: University of Miami Press, 1980.

The Original Floridians

Milanich, Jerald T., and Charles H. Fairbanks. *Florida Archaeology*. New York: Academic Press, 1980.

Milanich, Jerald T. *Florida's Indians from Ancient Times to the Present*. Gainesville: University Press of Florida, 2000.

Wright, J. Leitch, Jr. *The Only Land They Knew: The Tragic Story of the American Indians in the Old South*. New York: Free Press, 1981.

Discovery and Exploration (1513–1565)

Núñez Cabeza de Vaca, Alvar. *La "Relación" o "Naufragios" de Alvar Núñez Cabeza de Vaca*. Edited by Martin A. Favata and José B. Fernández. Potomac, Md.: Scripta Humanistica, 1986.

Milanich, Jerald T., and Charles Hudson. *Hernando de Soto and the Indians of Florida*. Gainesville: University Press of Florida, 1993.

Morison, Samuel Eliot. *The European Discovery of America: The Southern Voyages, A.D. 1492–1616*. New York: Oxford University Press, 1974.

Sauer, Carl O. *Sixteenth-Century North America: The Land and the People as Seen by the Europeans*. Berkeley: University of California Press, 1971.

First Spanish Period (1565–1763)

Bushnell, Amy Turner. *Situado and Sabana: Spain's Support System for the Presidio and Mission Provinces of Florida*. New York: American Museum of Natural History, 1994.

Deagan, Kathleen A. *Spanish St. Augustine: The Archaeology of a Colonial Creole Community*. New York: Academic Press, 1983.

Gannon, Michael V. *The Cross in the Sand: The Early Catholic Church in Florida, 1513–1870*. Gainesville: University of Florida Press, 1965.

Hann, John H. *Apalachee: The Land Between the Rivers*. Gainesville: University of Florida Press, 1988.

Hann, John H. *A History of the Timucua Indians and Missions*. Gainesville: University Press of Florida, 1996.

Landers, Jane. *Black Society in Spanish Florida*. Urbana: University of Illinois Press, 1999.

Lyon, Eugene. *The Enterprise of Florida: Pedro Menéndez de Avilés and the Spanish Conquest of 1565–1568*. Gainesville, University of Florida Press, 1976.

TePaske, John Jay. *The Governorship of Spanish Florida, 1700–1763*. Durham, N.C.: Duke University Press, 1964.

Weber, David J. *The Spanish Frontier in North America*. New Haven: Yale University Press, 1992.

Weddle, Robert S. *The Spanish Sea: The Gulf of Mexico in North American Discovery, 1500–1685*. College Station: Texas A&M University Press, 1985.

British Florida (1763–1784)

Coker, William S., and Robert R. Rea, eds. *Anglo-Spanish Confrontation on the Gulf Coast during the American Revolution*. Pensacola, Fla.: Gulf Coast History and Humanities Conference, 1982.

Fabel, Robin F. A. *The Economy of British West Florida, 1763–1783*. Tuscaloosa: University of Alabama Press, 1988.

Schafer, Daniel L. *St. Augustine's British Years, 1763–1784*. St. Augustine: St. Augustine Historical Society, 2001.

Wright, J. Leitch, Jr. *Florida in the American Revolution*. Gainesville: University of Florida Press, 1975.

Second Spanish Period (1784–1821)

Coker, William S., and Thomas D. Watson. *Indian Traders of the Southeastern Spanish Borderlands: Panton, Leslie and Company and John Forbes and Company. 1783–1847*. Gainesville: University of Florida Press, 1986.

Gordon, Elsbeth K. *Florida's Colonial Architectural Heritage*. Gainesville: University Press of Florida, 2002.

Patrick, Rembert W. *Florida Fiasco: Rampant Rebels on the Georgia-Florida Border, 1810–1815*. Athens: University of Georgia Press, 1954.

Tanner, Helen Hornbeck. *Zéspedes in East Florida, 1784–1790*. Coral Gables: University of Miami Press, 1963.

Territorial Florida (1821–1845)

Doherty, Herbert J. *Richard Keith Call, Southern Unionist.* Gainesville: University of Florida Press, 1961.

Mahon, John K. *History of the Second Seminole War, 1835–1842.* Rev. ed. Gainesville: University of Florida Press, 1985.

Smith, Julia Floyd. *Slavery and Plantation Growth in Antebellum Florida, 1821–1860.* Gainesville: University of Florida Press, 1973.

Thompson, Arthur W. *Jacksonian Democracy on the Florida Frontier.* Gainesville: University of Florida Press, 1961.

Statehood, Civil War, Reconstruction, and Gilded Age (1845–1900)

Ackerman, Joe A., Jr. *Florida Cowman: A History of Florida Cattle Raising.* Kissimmee: Florida Cattlemen's Association, 1976.

Akin, Edward N. *Flagler, Rockefeller Partner and Florida Baron.* Gainesville: University Press of Florida, 1992.

Graham, Thomas. *The Awakening of St. Augustine: The Anderson Family and the Oldest City, 1821–1924.* St. Augustine: St. Augustine Historical Society, 1978.

Johns, John E. *Florida during the Civil War.* Gainesville: University of Florida Press, 1963.

Nulty, William H. *Confederate Florida: The Road to Olustee.* Tuscaloosa: University of Alabama Press, 1990.

Peters, Thelma. *Lemon City: Pioneering on Biscayne Bay, 1850–1925.* Miami: Banyan Books, 1976.

Shofner, Jerrell. *Nor Is It Over Yet: Florida in the Era of Reconstruction, 1863–1877.* Gainesville: University of Florida Press, 1974.

Williamson, Edward C. *Florida Politics in the Gilded Age, 1877–1893.* Gainesville: University of Florida Press, 1976.

Twentieth Century

Colburn, David R. *Racial Change and Community Crisis: St. Augustine, Florida, 1877–1980.* Gainesville: University Press of Florida, 1991.

Flynt, Wayne. *Cracker Messiah: Governor Sidney J. Catts of Florida*. Baton Rouge: Louisiana State University Press, 1977.

Garbarino, Merwyn S. *Big Cypress, A Changing Seminole Community*. New York: Holt, Rinehart and Winston, 1972.

Kallina, Edward. *Claude Kirk and the Politics of Confrontation*. Gainesville: University Press of Florida, 1993.

Key, V[aldimer] O., Jr. *Southern Politics in State and Nation*. New York: Alfred A. Knopf, 1949.

McGovern, James R. *Anatomy of a Lynching: The Killing of Claude Neal*. Baton Rouge: Louisiana State University Press, 1982.

Mormino, Gary, and George E. Pozzetta. *The Immigrant World of Ybor City: Italians and Their Latin Neighbors in Tampa, 1885–1985*. Urbana: University of Illinois Press, 1987.

Nolan, David. *Fifty Feet in Paradise: The Booming of Florida*. San Diego, Calif.: Harcourt Brace Jovanovich, 1984.

Proctor, Samuel. *Napoleon Bonaparte Broward, Florida's Fighting Democrat*. Gainesville: University of Florida Press, 1950. Reprint: University Press of Florida, 1993.

Wagy, Thomas R. *Governor LeRoy Collins of Florida: Spokesman of the New South*. Tuscaloosa: University of Alabama Press, 1985.

Wall, Joseph Frazier. *Alfred I. du Pont: The Man and His Family*. New York: Oxford University Press, 1990.

INDEX

Page numbers in italics refer to pictures and captions.

Eighteenth Amendment, 74, 75
Ellis, Alpheus L., 122
English settlers. *See* British settlers
Environmental concerns, 85, 145–46, 147–48
Environmental Protection, Department of, 155
Epcot Center, 138, *147*
Episcopalians (Anglican church), 39
Escambia County, 28
Ethnicity, 140–42. *See also* Immigration
Everglades, 155, 156; drainage of, 70, *73*; hurricanes in, 83, *84*; Native American use of, 2, 35; prohibition in, *75*; protection for, 146, 148, *149*; sugar industry in, *73*, 98, 100; Tamiami Trail through, 85
Everglades Club, Palm Beach, 80
Everglades National Park, *149*

Fairbanks, George R., 40, 150
Fatio, Louisa, *39*
Federal Emergency Relief Administration (FERA), 89, *91*
Fenn, Harry, *49*
Fernandina, 27, 31, *38*, 40, 42, 43, *59*, 62
Fernandina Beach, 105
Fernandina *East Floridian*, 40
Fern industry, *54*
Fifty-fourth Massachusetts Infantry Regiment, *44–45*
Finegan, Gen. Joseph, 43
First North Carolina Infantry Regiment, *44–45*
First Seminole War, 27, *29, 36*
Fisher, Carl, 77
Fishing, *132–33*
Flagler, Henry Morrison, 53, 55–59, *56, 58, 68–69*, 77, 92, 106, 113
Flagler College, 57
Fleming, Francis P., 53
Fletcher, Duncan, 94
Flint River, 22
Florida, naming of, 4, *5*
Florida Agricultural and Mechan-

ical College, University, *65*, 71
Florida Chamber of Commerce, 157
Florida East Coast Railway Company (FEC), 57–58, *68–69*, 77, 89, *98*, 99, 124
Florida Gazette, 37
Florida Historical Society, 150–51
Florida National Bank, 122
Florida National Guard, 101, 104, 148
Florida Normal and Industrial Institute, 71
Florida Power and Light Company, 122
Florida Railroad, *38, 59*
Florida Southern College, 71, 113
Florida State College for Women, 71
Florida State Normal Industrial School, *65*, 71
Florida State Road Department, 119
Florida State University, 37, 71
Florida Straits, 105
Florida Turnpike, 119
Forbes land grant, 32
Forest products. *See* Pencil industry; Timber industry; Turpentine
Fort Barrancas (San Carlos), *41*, 42
Fort Caroline, 7, 8, *9*
Fort Clinch, 42
Fort Francis Marion. *See* Castillo de San Marcos (Fort Francis Marion)
Fort Gibson, Arkansas, 32
Fort George Island, 30
Fort Jefferson, 42
Fort King, 32
Fort Lauderdale, 64, *84*, 104
Fort Marion. *See* Castillo de San Marcos
Fort McRee, *41*, 42
Fort Mose, 16
Fort Myers, 43, 64, 80, 104, *108*, 140
Fort Pickens, *41*, 42, 150
Fort Pierce, 64, *117*, 140
Fort St. Marks, 27

in, 71, 119; aviation in, *69*, 104;
Cuban immigration to, *133*, 142;
development of, 58–59, 64,
77–82, *78–79*, *83*, 85, 118; drug-re-
lated crimes in, 146; hurricanes
in, 83, *84*, 145; Jewish immigration to, 140, *141*; police in, 81;
prohibition in, *75*, 76–77, *83*;
railroad service to, 77; during
Spanish-American War, 62
Miami Beach: architecture of, 113,
147; development of, 77, *78–79*;
hurricanes in, 83; Jewish immi-
gration to, 140, *141*; POW la-
borers in, 106; tourism in, 92;
troops training at, *102–3*
Miami Beach Post Office, 6
Miami-Dade County, 153, 154
Miami *Daily News*, 79
Miami–Fort Lauderdale–Palm
Beach megalopolis, 143
Miami Herald, 143
Miami River, 58
Miami Seaquarium, 138
Micanopy (Seminole chief), 31
Micanopy (town), 31
Middleton, Arthur, 24
Migrant (transient) workers, 73, 92,
96–97, 100, 120
Milton, John, 46
Minimum Foundation Program,
110, 123
Minorcan immigrants, 20–21, 140
Mirasol, El (house), Palm Beach, *82*
Missionaries: colonial settlement
by, 7, 8, 10–14, 17, 39; during
Reconstruction, 48
Mississippi (state): de Soto expedi-
tion in, *6*; lynchings in, 86; seces-
sion of, 41
Mississippi River, 17, *25*
Mitchell, Henry L., 53
Mixson, Wayne, 148
Mizner, Addison, 80, *82*, 113
Mobile, Alabama, 14, 20, 24, *25*, *35*
Moore, James, 14, 22, 26
Moore, Sara Grace, *65*
Moore Haven, 83
Morehouse, Ward, *101*
Moseley, William D., 37

Mosquito control, 108
Moultrie, John, 20
Moultrie Creek, 32
Muscogee, 26

Naples, 140, 144, 151
Narváez, Pánfilo de, 6
Nassau County, 39, 76
Nassau River, 24
Natchez, Mississippi, 20, *25*
National Airlines, Inc., 99
National Association for the Ad-
vancement of Colored People
(NAACP), *116*
National Youth Administration
(NYA), 89
Native Americans: under British
rule, 21–22; as first settlers, 1–3,
6; and missionaries, 10, 11, *12*,
14; refusal to be confined on
reservations, 52; remains of, 150;
removal of, 32–35; under
Spanish rule, 8, 16–17; under
territorial rule, 29–30. *See also*
Seminoles
Natural Bridge, 43
Naval Air Station, Pensacola, 104
Neill, Ella ("Miss Ella"), 93–94
New Deal, 89–95, 99, 124
Newfoundland, 4
New Orleans, Louisiana, 27, *35*
New Smyrna (plantation), 20
New Smyrna (town), 31
New South, 127
Newspapers, 37–38. *See also names
of individual newspapers*
New York Public Library, *58*
Nicaraguan immigrants, 142
Nombre de Dios (mission), 10
North Carolina: de Soto expedition
in, *6*; immigration to Florida
from, *47*; population of, 118;
slavery in, 19

Ocala, 31, 32, 37, 70, 140
Ocala Demands, 70
Ochlockonee Bay, *91*
Ocoee, 86
Oglethorpe, James Edward, 16

Pratt and Whitney, 138
Presbyterians, 39
Preston, Robert, *103*
Progressive movement, 67
Prohibition, *75*, 75–77
Public Works Administration (PWA), 89
Puerto Rico, *5*, 15; Spanish settlement of, 4
Punta Rassa, *60*

Quigg, H. Leslie, 81

Racism, 86–88, *128*
Radical Republicans, 48
Radio Corporation of America (RCA), 123
Raiford prison, 86, *87*
Railroads, 40, *47*, 53, *55*, 55–61, 77, 92, 98–99
Raleigh, Sir Walter, 4
Rawlings, Marjorie Kinnan, 113, *114–15*
Reapportionment, 135
Reconstruction, 46–53
Reed, Harrison, 48–49
Reed, Nathaniel, 154
Refrigeration, 40, 108
Reid, Robert Raymond, 36
Religion: churches established, 30, 38–39; and missionaries, 7, 8, 10–14, 17, 39; during Reconstruction, 47–48. *See also names of individual religious groups*
Republic of Mexico, 27
Republic of West Florida, 26
Retirees, 140
Ribault, Jean, 8
Rice, 20
Rinker, Marshall E., 122
River May, *7. See also* St. Johns River
Roads and highways, 30–31, *69*, 71, 92, 110, 119, 126–27, 144
Roaring Twenties, *83*
Robeson, Paul, *125*
Rockefeller, John D., 56
Rollins College, 71
Roman Catholic church, *21*, 39, 74;

and anti-Catholicism, 71, *73*, 74
Rommel, Erwin, 106
Roosevelt, Franklin D., 89, *90–91*, 92, 94, *99*
Roosevelt, Theodore D., 61
R[ío] S[an] Martín. *See* Suwannee
Rosenberg, Charles, 122
Rose Printing Company, 122
Rosewood, 86
Rough Riders, *61*, 61–62
Royal Air Force, British, 104
Royal Palm Hotel, Miami, 58
Royal Poinciana Hotel, Palm Beach, 58
Rural electrification, 70
Rutledge, Edward, 24

St. Andrews Bay, 43
St. Augustine: under American control, 28; aviation in, *69*; British settlement of, 18–19, 20, *23*, 24; as capital of East Florida, 18; churches in, 39; civil rights movement in, 131, *134*; during Civil War, 42; development of, 55, *58*, 63; fort at, *15*, 42; government in, 16; Governor's House at, *22*; importance of, 8, 30; mission Indians in, 14; name of, *19*; newspapers in, 24, 37; plan of, *21*; railroad service to, *56*; Spanish settlement of, 3, 4, *7*, *9*, 10, 15, 150; territorial legislature at, 28; trade with, 10, 17
St. Augustine Historical Society, *49*
St. Francis Street, St. Augustine, *49*
St. George Street, St. Augustine, *21*
St. Joe Paper Company, 95
St. Johns County, 28
St. Johns River, 2, 7, 8, 10, 20, 24, 30, 31, 64
St. Joseph, 30, 37
St. Louis and San Francisco railroad, 77
St. Lucie County, 144
St. Marks (town), 40
St. Marks River, 43

PICTURE CREDITS

The photographs, maps, and engravings included in this volume have been provided courtesy of the following collections or publications:

Pages 6, 18, 19, 21, 23, 25, 29, 31, 33, 34, 35, 38, 41, 47, 51, 52, 54, 55, 56, 58, 59, 60, 62, 64, 65, 66, 67, 68 (top and bottom), 72 (top and bottom), 75, 76, 78 (top and bottom), 81, 82, 83, 84, 87, 90 (top and bottom), 96 (top and bottom), 98, 99, 101, 102 (bottom), 108, 111, 114 (top and bottom), 116, 117, 120, 121, 125, 126, 128, 129, 134, 136, 137, 145, 147, 149: Florida State Archives.

Pages 15, 22, 39, 49, 57, 132 (top): St. Augustine Historical Society.

Pages 132 (bottom), 141: Historical Association of Southern Florida.

Page 61: Florida Historical Society Archives.

Page 102 (top): Library of Congress, Farm Security Administration.

Page 44: P. K. Yonge Library of Florida History.

Page 107: Collection of Reinhard Hardegen, Bremen, Germany.

Page 117: Special Collections, Rare Books and Literary Manuscripts, University of Florida Libraries.

Pages 2, 7: Stefan Lorant, ed., *The New World: The First Pictures of America, made by John White and Jacques LeMoyne and Engraved by Theodore de Bry, with Contemporary Narratives of the French Settlements in Florida, 1562–1565, and the English Colonies in Virginia, 1585–1590* (New York: Duell, Sloan, and Pearce, 1946).

Page 5: Edward W. Larson, *The Discovery of Florida and its Discoverer Juan Ponce de León* (St. Augustine, Florida: Edward W. Lawson, 1946).

Page 9: Eugene Lyon, *The Enterprise of Florida: Pedro Menéndez de Avilés and the Spanish Conquest of 1565–1568* (Gainesville: University of Florida Press, 1983).

Page 12: Mark F. Boyd, Hale G. Smith, and John W. Griffin, *Here They Once Stood: The Tragic End of the Apalachee Missions* (Gainesville: University of Florida Press, 1951).

Page 13: Michael V. Gannon, *The Cross in the Sand: The Early Catholic Church in Florida, 1513–1870* (Gainesville: University of Florida Press, 1965).

Page 198: John E. Johns, *Florida During the Civil War* (Gainesville: University of Florida Press, 1963).

Michael Gannon is Distinguished Service Professor Emeritus of History at the University of Florida, where he has taught the colonial history of Florida for a third of a century. His writings are familiar to many Florida readers in such books as *The New History of Florida* (UPF, 1996) and the bestselling *Operation Drumbeat*. In 1991, in recognition of Dr. Gannon's work in Spanish Florida studies, King Juan Carlos I of Spain awarded him the decoration Knight Commander of the Order of Isabel la Católica.